ATHENS

written and researched by

JOHN FISHER

Contents

<< FRIEZE, SIPHNIAN TREASURY, DELPHI
< PORCH OF THE CARYATIDS

INTRODUCTION TO
ATHENS

For all too many people, Athens is a city that happened two-and-a-half thousand years ago. It's true that even now the past looms large – literally, in the shape of the mighty Acropolis that dominates almost every view, as well as in every visitor's itinerary. Yet modern Athens is home to over four million people – more than a third of the Greek nation's population – and has undergone a radical transformation in the twenty-first century. The stimulus of the 2004 Olympics made it far more than a repository of antiquities, lifting the city above the clichés of pollution and impossible traffic that long blighted its reputation and giving rise to a regenerated city, whose vibrant street life rivals that of the liveliest European capitals.

STATUE OF POSEIDON, NATIONAL ARCHEOLOGICAL MUSEUM

Best places for a view of Athens

Athens is a city built on hills. Most famous is the **Acropolis** itself, which forms the backdrop to all the finest views of the city and whose summit also offers wonderful vistas across the metropolis and out to Pireás and the sea. But there are dozens of other viewpoints throughout the city. Some of the finest views are from the café terraces of Thissío, packed in the early evening as the setting sun picks out the ancient monuments – try **Chocolat Café** (p.69) or dine on the roof at **Filistron** (p.69). There are other great views from the roof-top bar at the **Hotel Grande Bretagne** (p.76), **Lykavitós Hill** (p.99), **Odhós Eólou** (p.81), **45°** (p.72), and from **Filopáppou Hill** (p.63).

There's no denying that the stunning remains of the ancient Classical Greek city – represented most famously by the Parthenon – remain the highlight of any visit to Athens, along with the National Archeological Museum, the finest collection of Greek antiquities in the world. The majority of the several million visitors who pass through each year do no more, perhaps managing dinner in one of the romantic but touristy tavernas of Pláka. In doing so, they see little of the Athens Athenians know. Even on a brief visit, it doesn't do the city justice to see it purely as a collection of ancient sites and museum pieces.

It's worth taking the time to explore the city's neighbourhoods. For all its tourists, the nineteenth-century quarter of Pláka, with its mix of Turkish, Neoclassical and Greek island-style architecture, is perhaps the most easily appreciated. Just to the north, the bazaar area retains an almost Middle Eastern atmosphere, with the added bonus of some of the city's best nightlife in Psyrrí and up-and-coming Gázi. More traditional Athenian escapes are nearby, in the form of the shady National Gardens and upmarket Kolonáki. There are startling views to be enjoyed from the many hills – Lykavitós and Filopáppou in particular – while in summer, the beach is just a tram-ride away.

Further out, and easily reached on day-trips, are more Classical sites – Soúnio and Delphi above all – and opportunities to walk in the mountains, and to escape to the islands, several of which can be reached from the port of Pireás in little over an hour.

The biggest surprise in Athens for most people, however, is the vibrant life of the city itself. Cafés are packed day and night, and the streets stay lively until 3 or 4am, with no end of buzzing bars and clubs to choose from. Eating out is great, with establishments ranging from lively tavernas to the finest gourmet restaurants. In summer much of the action takes place outdoors, complemented by open-air films, concerts and classical drama. There's a diverse shopping scene, too, ranging from colourful bazaars and lively street markets to chic shopping malls filled with the latest designer goods. And with a good-value, extensive public transport system, as well as inexpensive cabs, you'll have no difficulty getting around.

When to visit

Athens is at its most agreeable outside the peak period of **early July** to the end of **August**, when soaring temperatures (sometimes over 40°C), plus crowds of visitors, can be overpowering. Perhaps the best months to visit are **May to early June**, **September** and **October** – temperatures are pleasant (20°C and upwards), and visitors fewer. In **April** you can see lovely displays of spring flowers in the surrounding mountains. The **winter** months can be very cold, and February is often rainy, but they have their attractions too, in cosy restaurants and bars and the chance, on clear wintry days, to see the sights in fabulous light and almost empty of tourists.

THISSIO NIGHTLIFE

ATHENS AT A GLANCE

>>EATING

Greek food, with its fresh ingredients and simple, robust flavours, is a great deal better than generally acknowledged, and in Athens you'll find the finest of it, both traditional and with a modern twist. In the centre, the touristy tavernas of **Pláka** offer plenty of romance, though you'll eat more authentically and cheaply in the neighbouring district of **Monastiráki** or with much more style in fashionable **Psyrrí** or **Gázi**. For a real taste of traditional Greek cuisine and hospitality, though, it's best to escape the centre altogether and head for the tavernas in areas like **Exárhia**, or the entirely untouristed neighbourhoods of **Áno Petrálona** or **Pangráti**.

>>DRINKING

Athenians are obsessive about **cafés** and there seems to be one on every corner, busy at almost any time of day. The drink of choice in summer is **frappé** – whisked, iced, instant coffee (much better than it sounds) – or its more sophisticated cousin cappuccino freddo. These places also serve alcoholic drinks at any time of day, and many transform themselves in the evening into chilled-out **lounge bars**. Actual bars are much more scarce, and most open late, as the town revs up towards its early-hours nightlife.

>>SHOPPING

Shopping in Athens is decidedly schizophrenic. On the one hand the **bazaar area** is an extraordinary jumble of little specialist shops and stalls, while almost every neighbourhood still hosts a weekly **street market**. On the other, the upmarket shopping areas, Kolonáki especially, and the **malls** and fashion emporia of the ritzier suburbs like Kifissiá and Glyfádha are as glossy and expensive as any in Europe. Somewhere between the extremes you'll find endless **stoas**, covered arcades full of little shops. Some have been expensively refurbished; most, though, are a little dilapidated, and many still specialize in a single product – books here, computer equipment there, spectacles in another.

>>NIGHTLIFE

When it comes to nightlife, Athens is a very different place in winter – the best time to catch live music – than in summer. There are clubs throughout the city, but the most vibrant nightlife is in and around **Psyrrí**, **Gázi** and **Thissío**. In high summer many bars and clubs move out of the city centre to escape the heat and into temporary beachfront homes in the coastal suburbs. One quintessentially Greek experience not to miss is an **outdoor movie**; in summer screens spring up in every neighbourhood of the city.

OUR RECOMMENDATIONS FOR WHERE TO EAT, DRINK AND SHOP ARE LISTED AT THE END OF EACH CHAPTER.

Day One in Athens

1 The Parthenon > p.32. This iconic sight can be hard to appreciate through the crowds, so try to come early.

2 Theatre of Dionysos > p.35. Only a part of the birthplace of Classical drama survives intact, but this is impressive enough. From here you can complete a circuit of the Acropolis.

3 Acropolis Museum > p.34. The magnificent new building does more than justice to its contents.

🍴 Lunch > p.39. The *Acropolis Museum Café* serves the best-value light lunch in Athens, with delicious modern Greek flavours and stunning views.

4 Pláka > p.40. Stroll through the old district of Pláka, full of cafés, souvenir shops and quirky hidden corners.

5 Roman Forum > p.46. The Romans as well as the ancient Greeks left their mark on Athens; this was the heart of their town.

6 Ancient Agora > p.37. The sprawling remains of the Ancient Agora, the Greek marketplace, complete a circuit of the city-centre monuments.

7 Sunset > p.69. Cool off with a frappé or beer at a Thissío café, as the rays of the setting sun bathe the Acropolis in front of you. *Chocolat Café* also serves great cocktails.

🍴 Dinner > p.60. Athenians eat late, so head for the buzz of Psyrrí after 9pm and join the crowds. *Taverna tou Psyrri* is at the heart of the action.

Day Two in Athens

1 **National Archeological Museum**
> p.89. Simply the finest collection of
ancient Greek artefacts anywhere in
the world.

2 **The bazaar** > p.80. Take in the
sights and smells of the meat and
seafood market; across the road are
fruit and vegetables, while all around
are the extraordinary, antiquated
emporia of the bazaar area.

3 **Odhós Eólou** > p.81. This
pedestrianized shopping street was the
approach to Athens in ancient times –
admire the views as you enjoy a frappé
at a street café.

Lunch > p.58. Off Platía
Monastirakíou are some of
the busiest and most traditional lunch
spots in Athens – none more so than
Baïraktaris.

4 **Benáki Museum of Islamic Art**
> p.66. A beautiful, fascinating little
museum that serves as a reminder of
a little-known Athenian era.

5 **Kerameikos** > p.66. One of
classical Athens' principal burial
grounds occupies a still-peaceful spot
just outside the ancient city walls.

6 **Filopáppou Hill** > p.63. An easy
stroll up wooded paths to a marvellous
viewpoint over city and sea.

Dinner > p.70. Áno
Petrálona is an untouristed
neighbourhood, close to the city
centre, whose authentic, inexpensive
tavernas attract plenty of locals.
At *Ikonomou* you may have trouble
interpreting the waiter's description of
what's on offer, but whatever you have,
it will be good.

Budget Athens

The sights and sounds of Athens' streets and markets cost nothing, and almost all come with the breathtaking backdrop of the Acropolis. In winter, many of the city's sites and museums are free on Sunday.

1 #400 bus > p.154. For just €5, this hop-on, hop-off service will shuttle you around the city's main sights all day – with commentary. And the ticket includes free use of all other public transport for 24 hours.

2 Museum of Greek Popular Musical Instruments > p.45. A lovely, offbeat little museum. Best of all, it's free.

3 Platía Syndágmatos > p.74. There's always something going on in the city's main square, from the changing of the guard in front of the parliament to almost daily marches and demos. The city provides free wi-fi here too.

4 National Gardens > p.76. A shady respite from the summer heat, and a lovely place for a stroll.

🍴 **Lunch** > p.79. Pick up a tyrópita at *Ariston* or a sandwich from *Everest*, and picnic on a bench in the National Gardens.

5 Platía Klafthomónos > p.83. Bustling square in the heart of business Athens, and a fascinating glimpse of how the city might have been.

6 Edem Beach > p.188. Hop on the tram and head down to this free beach, where you can swim in remarkably clean water and be back in the centre in the space of just a couple of hours.

7 Lykavitós > p.99. They charge for the funicular, but it costs nothing to walk to the top of Lykavitós Hill for some of the city's most spectacular views, especially fine at dusk.

🍴 **Dinner** > p.95. In the heart of studenty Exárhia, *To Indiko tou Barba George* serves up cheap-and-cheerful curries.

Unknown Athens

For all its tourist crowds, there are plenty of corners of Athens that are barely visited or known only to locals.

5 **Áyios Dhimítrios** > p.64. Athens' Byzantine churches are often overlooked by visitors; this is a lovely and historic example in a peaceful spot.

6 **Pireás** > p.117. Hardly unknown, but few people come here to admire the place; yet the constant traffic of ferries and hydrofoils is mesmerizing and there's an excellent Archeological Museum near the tranquil small-boat harbours.

1 **Peripatos** > p.36. This newly opened trail around the back of the Acropolis is discovered only by a few visitors; appropriately, you can spot the secret path that the ancients used to climb to the top undetected.

2 **Athens University Museum** > p.44. Little-visited even by locals, this lovely old mansion is free to enter and has fabulous views.

3 **Turkish Baths** > p.45. Lovely restoration of the ancient *hamam*, illuminating an era of Athenian history that is often passed over.

Lunch > p.86. Descending into the obscure basement near the market that houses *Dhiporto* feels like stepping back into an Athens of forty years ago.

4 **Iridhanós river** > p.54. Lost for centuries after being rerouted underground, the river was uncovered again during work on the Metro.

Drinks > p.126. Head down the coast from Pireás to Glyfádha, for drinks at *Cosi*. Packed with locals, Athens' summer playground barely registers on most visitors' radar.

Dinner > p.127. Still in Glyfádha, *George's Steak House* offers more of the same: crowds of locals with barely a tourist in sight.

Eating

1 Café Abysinia With its modern twists on classic Greek dishes, *Café Abysinia* offers a hugely popular alternative eating experience. **> p.58**

2 Ammos A fishy lunch overlooking a picturesque harbour in Pireás is an essential part of an Athenian weekend. > **p.127**

3 Taverna Ikonomou A wonderful neighbourhood taverna in a part of Athens rarely visited by tourists. > **p.70**

4 Psyrrí Thronged every night till late, *To Souvlaki tou Psyrri* is one of the most popular of Psyrrí's numerous restaurants. > **p.60**

5 Barba Yiannis Choose your food from the trays on display and your wine from the barrel; living Athenian tradition. > **p.94**

Nightlife

1 Cubanita Party all night at this Latin music spot; a prime example of Psyrrí's vibrant nightlife. > **p.61**

2 Gázi Gázi is the heart of Athens' club scene, with new venues seeming to spring up every week alongside the more established clubs, such as the lively 45°. > **p.73**

4 To Baraki tou Vasili Traditional Greek music every night, featuring contemporary greats as well as the stars of the future. > **p.109**

3 Odhós Miaoúli This street leading up from the metro station to the heart of Psyrrí is packed with bars whose tables spill out across the pavements; meet here before heading on to a club. > **p.60**

5 Micra Asia The roof terrace of this chilled-out bar offers an escape from the wilder Gázi clubbing scene. > **p.72**

Shopping and markets

1 Elixirion A wonderfully old-fashioned store, surrounded by the old curiosity shops of the bazaar. > **p.84**

4 Crop Circle A typically alternative Exárhia store, selling both new and vintage clothing and jewellery. > **p.93**

2 Boutiques and designer malls To shop like a local, head for the glitzy designer stores and upmarket malls of Kolonáki, Glyfádha or Kifissiá. > **p.105** & **p.126**

5 Monastiráki Flea Market The name may be misleading, but this is still the place for some of the most interesting shopping in Athens. > **p.56**

3 Street markets Every neighbourhood of Athens still has a weekly street market, whose fresh produce is a visual treat even if you're not buying. > **p.93**, **p.105** & **p.113**

Café life

1 Da Capo Just off Platía Kolonakíou, *Da Capo* is right at the heart of upmarket Athenian café culture. > **p.106**

2 Frappé An iced frappé is the quintessential taste of a Greek summer. Don't leave Athens without trying one. > **p.7**

3 Glyfádha The glossy cafés in the beachside suburb of Glyfádha are busy with shoppers year-round; in summer, they're packed all night. > **p.126**

4 Athinaion Politeia A terrace with magical views of the Acropolis makes this a great place to relax over a cold drink – especially at sunset. > **p.69**

5 Glykis A quiet, locals' escape in touristy Pláka. > **p.49**

Museums

1 Acropolis Museum State-of-the-art new museum, where the building, café and political statement threaten to outshine the objects on display. **> p.34**

2 Benaki Museum of Islamic Art Offering a very different perspective on Athens, this tranquil space is filled with objects of exceptional beauty. **> p.66**

3 Byzantine & Christian Museum
Highlights are the religious art – gorgeous icons and whole frescoes, rescued from the walls of ancient chapels. **> p.103**

4 Museum of Greek Folk Art
An enjoyable jumble of art, clothing, jewellery, crafts and more. **> p.41**

5 National Archeological Museum
One of the world's great museums. The magnificent gold funerary "Mask of Agamemnon" is just one of the many highlights. **> p.89**

23

The Acropolis and Makriyiánni

The rock of the Acropolis, crowned by the dramatic ruins of the Parthenon, is one of the archetypal images of Western culture. The first time you see it, rising above the traffic or from a distant hill, is extraordinary: foreign and yet utterly familiar. The Parthenon temple was always intended to be a landmark, and was famous throughout the ancient world. Yet even in their wildest dreams its creators could hardly have imagined that the ruins would come to symbolize the emergence of Western civilization – nor that, two-and-a-half millennia on, it would attract some three million tourists a year.

The **Acropolis** itself is simply the rock on which the monuments are built; almost every ancient Greek city had its acropolis (which means the summit or highest point of the city), but the acropolis of Athens is The Acropolis, the one that needs no further introduction. Its natural setting, a steep-sided, flat-topped crag of limestone rising abruptly a hundred metres from its surroundings, has made it the focus of the city during every phase of its development. Easily defensible and with plentiful water, its initial attractions are obvious. Even now, with no function apart from tourism, it is the undeniable heart of the city, around which everything else clusters, glimpsed at almost every turn.

THE PARTHENON

Approaches to the Acropolis

You can walk an entire circuit of the Acropolis and Ancient Agora on pedestrianized streets, allowing them to be appreciated from almost every angle: in particular, the pedestrianization has provided spectacular new terraces for cafés to the west, in Thissío. On the other side, in Pláka, you may get a little lost among the jumble of alleys, but the rock itself is always there to guide you.

The **summit** of the Acropolis can be entered only from the west, where there's a big coach park at the bottom of the hill: **bus** #230 from Sýndagma will take you almost to the entrance. **On foot**, the obvious approach is from Metro Akrópoli to the south, along pedestrianized Dhionysíou Areopayítou past the new Acropolis Museum and South Slope (or through the South Slope site). **From Pláka** a path towards the entrance climbs above Odhós Dhioskoúron, or you can enter the North Slope fenced area from Odhós Theorías, by the Kanellopoulo Museum. **From the north** you can approach via the Ancient Agora (entrance on Adhrianoú; Metro Monastiráki); or, slightly further but repaid with excellent views of both Agora and Acropolis, from Thissío along traffic-free Apostólou Pávlou (Metro Thissío).

On top of the Acropolis stands the **Parthenon** along with the **Erechtheion**, the **Temple of Athena Nike** and the **Propylaia** – the gateway through which the ancient sanctuary was entered – as well as lesser remains of many other ancient structures. All of these are included in a single, fenced site. The **South Slope of the Acropolis**, with two great theatres and several smaller temples, has separate entrances and ticketing, as does the **Ancient Agora**, on the opposite side. A vast amount of reconstruction is going on, throughout the Acropolis sites – one benefit is excellent new signage, with thorough descriptions, pictures and reconstructions. Most impressive of all is the new **Acropolis Museum**, looking up at the Parthenon from the quiet, upmarket residential quarter of **Makriyiánni**.

There are no shops or restaurants within the Acropolis area, but you can buy water, sandwiches and postcards from the stands near the main ticket office. There's also a handy branch of the sandwich shop Everest right opposite Akrópoli metro station (at the corner of Makriyiánni and Dhiakoú) and plenty of similar places around Monastiráki metro. A couple of restaurants in Makriyiánni are listed on p.39, but there are also cafés and tavernas nearby in almost every direction: see Pláka (p.48), Monastiráki (p.58) and Thissío (p.69).

THE PROPYLAIA

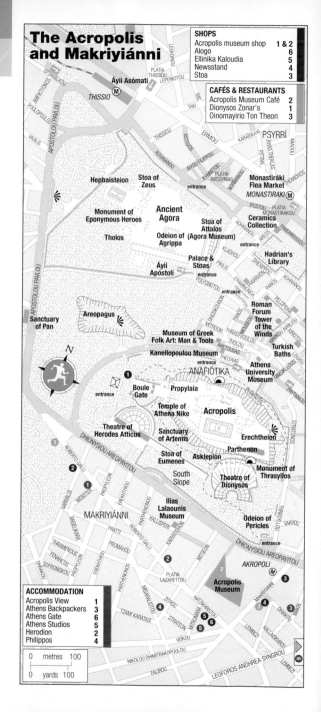

The Acropolis and Makriyiánni

SHOPS

Acropolis museum shop	1 & 2
Alogo	6
Ellinika Kaloudia	5
Newsstand	4
Stoa	3

CAFÉS & RESTAURANTS

Acropolis Museum Café	2
Dionysos Zonar's	1
Oinomayirio Ton Theon	3

ACCOMMODATION

Acropolis View	1
Athens Backpackers	3
Athens Gate	6
Athens Studios	5
Herodion	2
Philippos	4

0   metres   100
0   yards   100

THE PROPYLAIA

Main Acropolis site. MAP P.28, POCKET MAP B13

Today, as throughout history, the **Propylaia** are the gateway to the Acropolis. In Classical times the road extended along a steep ramp to this monumental double-gatehouse; the modern path makes a more gradual, zigzagging ascent, passing first through an arched Roman entrance, the Beule Gate, added in the third century AD.

THE PROPYLAIA

The Propylaia were constructed by Mnesikles between 437 BC and 432 BC, and their axis and proportions aligned to balance the recently completed Parthenon. They were built from the same marble as the temple, and in grandeur and architectural achievement are almost as impressive. The ancient Athenians, awed by the fact that such wealth and craftsmanship should be used for a purely secular building, ranked this as their most prestigious monument.

Walking through the gateway, which would originally have had great wooden doors, is your only chance to enter any of the ancient buildings atop the Acropolis. To the left of the central hall, part of whose great coffered roof has been restored (originally this was painted blue and gilded with stars), the **Pinakotheke** was an early art gallery, exhibiting paintings of Homeric subjects by Polygnotus. The wing to the right is much smaller, as Mnesikles's original design incorporated ground sacred to the Goddess of Victory and the premises had to be adapted as a waiting room for her shrine – the **Temple of Athena Nike**.

Acropolis tickets and opening times

A **joint ticket** (€12; free to under-18s and EU students; €6 for non-EU students; free on public holidays and Sundays Nov–March) covers the Acropolis, Ancient Agora and South Slope, plus the Roman Forum, Kerameikos and the Temple of Olympian Zeus. The smaller sites also offer individual tickets, but only the joint one is valid for the summit of the Acropolis, so if you visit any of the others first, be sure to buy the multiple ticket or you simply end up paying twice. The ticket can be used over four days. Backpacks and large bags are not allowed into the site – there's a cloakroom near the main ticket office.

The Acropolis, South Slope (individual entry €2) and Ancient Agora (individual entry €4) are **open** daily April to September 8am to 7.30pm, October to March 8.30am to 3pm. Crowds can be horrendous – to avoid the worst, come very early or late in the day.

Disabled access to the summit of the Acropolis is available via a lift on the north side (by arrangement only; ☎ 210 92 38 175).

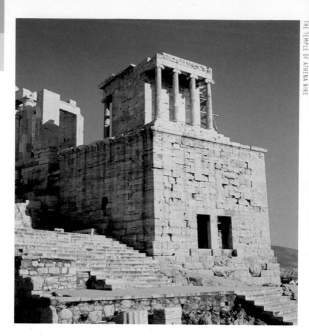

THE TEMPLE OF ATHENA NIKE

Main Acropolis site. MAP P.28, POCKET MAP B13

Simple and elegant, the Temple of Athena Nike stands on a precipitous platform alongside the Propylaia, overlooking the port of Pireás and the Saronic Gulf. It has only recently reappeared, having been dismantled, cleaned, restored and reconstructed, a process which is still not entirely finished. Not for the first time either: demolished by the Turks in the seventeenth century, the temple was reconstructed from its original blocks two hundred years later.

In myth, it was from the platform beside the temple that King Aegeus maintained a vigil for the safe return of his son Theseus from his mission to slay the Minotaur on Crete. Theseus, flushed with success, forgot his promise to swap the boat's black sails for white on his return. Seeing the black sails, Aegeus assumed his son had perished and, racked with grief, threw himself to his death.

THE PANATHENAIC WAY

Main Acropolis site. MAP P.28, POCKET MAP C13

The **Panathenaic Way** was the route of the great annual procession for ancient Athens' Panathenaic Festival, in honour of the city's patron goddess Athena. The procession – depicted on the Parthenon frieze – wound right through the Classical city from the gates now in the Kerameikos site (p.66) via the Propylaia to the Parthenon and, finally, the Erechtheion. You can see traces of the ancient route just inside the Propylaia, where there are grooves cut for footholds in the rock and, to either side, niches for innumerable statues and offerings. In Classical times it ran past a ten-metre-high bronze statue of Athena Promachos (Athena the Champion), whose base can just about be made out. Athena's spear and helmet were said to be visible to sailors approaching from as far away as Soúnio.

Close to the Propylaia too are the scant remains of a **Sanctuary of Artemis**.

Although its function remains obscure, it is known that the precinct once housed a colossal bronze representation of the Wooden Horse of Troy. More noticeable is a nearby stretch of **Mycenaean wall** (running parallel to the Propylaia) that was incorporated into the Classical design.

A brief history of the Acropolis

The rocky **Acropolis** was home to one of the earliest known settlements in Greece, its slopes inhabited by a Neolithic community around 5000 BC. In Mycenaean times – around 1500 BC – it was fortified with Cyclopean walls, parts of which can still be seen, enclosing a royal palace and temples to the goddess Athena. By the ninth century BC, the Acropolis had become the heart of Athens, the first Greek city-state, sheltering its principal public buildings.

Most of the substantial remains seen today date from the fifth century BC or later, by which time the buildings here were purely religious. Earlier temples and sanctuaries had been burned to the ground when the Persians sacked Athens in 480 BC. In 449 BC, with the war against Persia won, the walls were rebuilt and plans drawn up for a reconstruction worthy of the city's cultural and political ascendancy. This vast project, coinciding with the Golden Age of Classical Athens, was masterminded by **Pericles** and carried out under the general direction of the architect and sculptor **Fidias**. It was completed in an incredibly short time: the Parthenon itself took only ten years to finish.

The monuments survived barely altered for close to a thousand years, until in the reign of Emperor Justinian the temples were converted to Christian worship. Over the following centuries their uses became secular as well as religious, and embellishments increased, gradually obscuring the Classical designs. Fifteenth-century Italian princes held court in the Propylaia, and the same quarters were later used by the Turks as their commander's headquarters and as a powder magazine. The Parthenon underwent similar changes from Greek to Roman temple, from Byzantine church to Frankish cathedral, before several centuries of use as a Turkish mosque. The Erechtheion, with its graceful female figures, saw service as a harem.

The Acropolis buildings finally fell victim to war, blown up during successive attempts by the Venetians to oust the Turks. In 1684, the Turks demolished the Temple of Athena Nike to gain a brief tactical advantage. Three years later the Venetians, laying siege to the garrison, ignited a Turkish gunpowder magazine in the Parthenon, in the process blasting off its roof and starting a fire that raged for two days and nights. The process of stripping down to the bare ruins seen today was completed by souvenir hunters and the efforts of the first archeologists – see the box on p.33.

THE PARTHENON

THE PARTHENON

Main Acropolis site. MAP P.28, POCKET MAP C13

The **Parthenon** was the first great building in Pericles' scheme, intended as a sanctuary for Athena and a home for her cult image – a colossal wooden statue overlaid with ivory and gold plating, with precious gems as eyes and an ivory gorgon death's-head on her breast.

Originally the Parthenon was brightly painted and decorated with the finest sculpture of the Classical age. Of these, the best surviving examples are in the British Museum in London (see box opposite); the Acropolis Museum has others, but the greater part of the pediments, along with the central columns and the cella, were destroyed by the Venetian bombardment in 1687.

To achieve the Parthenon's extraordinary and unequalled harmony of design, its architect, Iktinos, used every trick known to the Doric order of architecture. Every ratio – length to width, width to height, and even such relationships as the distances between the columns and their diameter – is constant, while any possible appearance of disproportion is corrected by meticulous mathematics and craftsmanship. All seemingly straight lines are in fact slightly curved, an optical illusion known as *entasis* (intensification). The columns (their profile bowed slightly to avoid seeming concave) are slanted inwards by 6cm, while each of the steps along the sides of the temple was made to incline just 12cm over a length of 70m.

A scaffolder's dream

If you see a photo of a pristine Parthenon standing against a clear sky, it is almost certainly an old one. For most of the twenty-first century the Acropolis buildings have been swathed in scaffolding and surrounded by cranes. Though originally intended to be complete in time for the 2004 Olympics, the work is now set to continue for the foreseeable future – some claim that it will be forty years before the job is complete.

The Parthenon Marbles

The controversy over the so-called **Elgin Marbles** has its origin in the activities of Western looters at the start of the nineteenth century: above all the French ambassador Fauvel, gathering antiquities for the Louvre, and Lord Elgin. As British ambassador, Elgin obtained permission from the Turks to erect scaffolding, excavate and remove stones with inscriptions. He interpreted this as a licence to make off with almost all of the bas-reliefs from the Parthenon's frieze, most of its pedimental structures and a caryatid from the Erechtheion – all of which he later sold to the **British Museum**. While there were perhaps justifications for Elgin's action at the time – not least the Turks' tendency to use Parthenon stones in their lime kilns – his pilfering was controversial even then. Byron, for one, roundly disparaged his activities.

The Greeks hoped that the long-awaited completion of the new Acropolis Museum would create the perfect opportunity for the British Museum to bow to pressure and return the marbles. But despite a campaign begun by Greek actress and culture minister Melina Mercouri in the early 1980s, there is so far little sign of that happening.

THE ERECHTHEION

Main Acropolis site. MAP P.28, POCKET MAP C13

The **Erechtheion**, the last of Pericles' great works to be completed, was the most revered of the ancient temples. Both Athena and the city's old patron, Poseidon (known here as Erechtheus), were worshipped here. The site was that on which Athena and Poseidon held a contest, judged by their fellow Olympian gods: at the touch of Athena's spear, the first-ever olive tree sprang from the ground, while Poseidon summoned forth a fountain of sea water. Athena won, and became patron of the city.

Today, the sacred objects are long gone, but the elegant Ionic porticoes survive. The most striking feature is the famous **Porch of the Caryatids**, whose columns form the tunics of six tall maidens. The ones in situ are, sadly, replacements. Five of the originals are in the Acropolis Museum; a sixth was looted by Elgin (see box above).

THE ACROPOLIS MUSEUM

Enter from Dhionysíou Areopayítou 15
Ⓦ www.theacropolismuseum.gr. Tues–Sun
8am–8pm, last admission 7.30pm. €5.
MAP P.28, POCKET MAP C14

The new **Acropolis Museum**
is a magnificent building, filled
with beautiful objects, with a
wonderful sense of space and
light and a glass top storey
with a direct view up to the
Parthenon itself.

The remains of ancient
Athens uncovered during
building work can be seen even
before you enter, protected
under glass flooring and an
external canopy; more can be
seen under glass beneath your
feet throughout the ground
floor. The displays start with a
ramp described as the **Slopes
of the Acropolis**, as that is
where most of the pottery and
other objects displayed here
were found. At the top of the
ramp are sculptures from the
pediment of an early temple
that stood on the site of the
Parthenon, the Hekatompedon.
Their surviving paintwork
gives a good indication of the
vivid colours originally used in
temple decoration.

On the **first floor**, statues
predominate: the *Moscho-
phoros*, a painted marble statue

of a young man carrying a
sacrificial calf, dated 570 BC,
is one of the earliest examples
of Greek art in marble. There's
also an extensive collection of
Korai, or statues of maidens.
The progression in style, from
the simply contoured Doric
clothing to the more elegant
and voluminous Ionic designs,
is fascinating; the figures' smiles
also change subtly, becoming
increasingly loose and natural.

On the **top floor**, a fifteen-
minute video (alternately in
English and Greek) offers a
superb introduction to the
Parthenon sculptures. The
metopes and the frieze are set
out around the outside of the
hall, arranged as they would
have been on the Parthenon
itself; the pediments are
displayed separately at each end
of the gallery. Only a relatively
small number are original
(see box, p.33); the rest are
represented by plaster copies
which seem deliberately crude,
to make a point (there are
better copies in Akropoli metro
station, for example).

On the way back down
through the museum are
statues from the Temple
of Athena Nike and the
Erectheion, including the

34

original Caryatids. The sculptures from the parapet of the former, all depicting Athena Nike in various guises, include a particularly graceful and fluid sculpture known as *Iy Sandalizomeni*, which depicts her adjusting her sandal.

THEATRE OF DIONYSOS

South Slope site. MAP P.28, POCKET MAP C14

The **Theatre of Dionysos** is one of the most evocative locations in the city. Here the masterpieces of Aeschylus, Sophocles, Euripides and Aristophanes were first performed; it was also the venue in Classical times for the annual festival of tragic drama, where each Greek citizen would take his turn as member of the chorus. Rebuilt in the fourth century BC, the theatre could hold some 17,000 spectators – considerably more than Herodes Atticus's 5000–6000 seats; twenty of the original 64 tiers of seats survive.

HERODES ATTICUS THEATRE

South Slope site. MAP P.28, POCKET MAP B14

The dominant structure on the south side of the Acropolis – much more immediately obvious even than the Theatre of Dionysos – is the second-century Roman **Herodes Atticus Theatre** (Odeion of Herodes Atticus). Extensively restored for performances of music and Classical drama during the **summer festival** (see p.158) it is open only for shows; at other times you'll have to be content with spying over the wall.

STOA OF EUMENES

South Slope site. MAP P.28, POCKET MAP C14

Between the two theatres lie the foundations of the **Stoa of Eumenes**, originally a massive colonnade of stalls erected in the second century BC. Above the stoa, high up under the walls of the Acropolis, extend the ruins of the **Asklepion**, a sanctuary devoted to the healing god Asklepios and built around a sacred spring.

MONUMENT OF THRASYLLOS

South Slope site. MAP P.28, POCKET MAP C14

Above the Theatre of Dionysos, you can see the entry to a huge cave, originally sacred to Artemis. It later housed choregic awards (to celebrate victory in drama contests; see Monument of Lysikratos, p.43) won by the family of Thrasyllos, and its entrance was closed off around 320 BC with a marble facade (currently being restored). The cave was later converted to Christian use and became the Chapel of the Virgin Mary of the Rocks, but an ancient statue of Dionysos remained inside until it was removed by Lord Elgin (it's now in the British Museum), while the Classical structure survived almost unchanged until 1827, when it was blown up in a Turkish siege.

HERODES ATTICUS THEATRE

THE PERIPATOS

South slope site. MAP P.28, POCKET MAP C14

The **Peripatos** was the ancient street that ran around the north side of the Acropolis. Access to this side has only recently been opened up so that you can now walk right around the rock within the fenced site, starting above the Theatre of Dionysos and emerging by the entry to the main Acropolis site; there's also a new entrance from Pláka, by the Kannellopoulou museum.

There are no major monuments en route, but the numerous caves and springs help explain the strategic importance of the Acropolis. In one impressive cleft in the rock was a secret stairway leading up to the temples: this provided access to spring-water in times of war, and was also used in rituals, when blindfolded initiates would be led this way. Nearby are numerous other caves and rock arches that had cult status in ancient times.

THE AREOPAGUS

Immediately below the entrance to the Acropolis. MAP P.28, POCKET MAP B13

Metal steps as well as ancient, slippery, rock-hewn stairs ascend the low, unfenced hill of the **Areopagus**. The "Hill of Ares" was the site of the Council of Nobles and the Judicial Court under the aristocratic rule of ancient Athens. During the Classical period the court lost its powers of government to the Assembly (held on the Pnyx) but it remained the court of criminal justice.

In myth, this was also the site where Ares, God of War, was tried for the murder of one of Poseidon's sons; Aeschylus used the setting in *The Eumenides* for the trial of Orestes, who stood accused of murdering his mother Clytemnestra. The Persians camped here during their siege of the Acropolis in 480 BC, and in the Roman era St Paul preached the "Sermon on an Unknown God" on the hill, winning amongst his converts Dionysios "the Areopagite", who became the city's patron saint.

Today, there's little evidence of ancient grandeur beyond various steps and niches cut into the perilously slippery rock, and the hill is littered with cigarette butts and empty beer-cans left by the crowds who come to rest after their exertions on the Acropolis and

VIEW FROM THE AREOPAGUS

to enjoy the **views**. These, at least, are good – down over the Agora and towards the ancient cemetery of Kerameikos.

THE ANCIENT AGORA

Ancient Agora site. MAP P.28, POCKET MAP B12
The **Agora** or market was the heart of ancient Athenian city life from as early as 3000 BC. Today, the site is an extensive and rather confusing jumble of ruins, dating from various stages of building between the sixth century BC and the fifth century AD. As well as the marketplace, the Agora was the chief meeting-place of the city, where orators held forth, business was discussed and gossip exchanged. It was also the original home of the democratic assembly, and continued to be its meeting place when cases of ostracism were discussed for most of the Classical period.

The best overview of the site is from the exceptionally well-preserved **Hephaisteion**, or Temple of Hephaistos, where there's a terrace overlooking the rest of the site from the west. The observation point here has a plan showing the buildings as they were in 150 AD, and the various remains laid out in front of you make a lot more sense with this to help (there are similar plans at the entrances). The temple itself was originally thought to be dedicated to Theseus, because his exploits are depicted on the frieze (hence Thission, which has given its name to the area); more recently it has been accepted that it actually honoured Hephaistos, patron of blacksmiths and metal-workers. It was one of the earliest buildings of Pericles' programme, but also one of the least known – perhaps because it lacks the curvature and "lightness" of the Parthenon's design. The barrel-vaulted roof dates from a Byzantine conversion into the church of St George.

The other church on the site – that of **Áyii Apóstoli** (the Holy Apostles), by the south entrance – is worth a look as you wander among the extensive foundations of the other Agora buildings. Inside are fragments of fresco, exposed during restoration of the eleventh-century shrine.

37

THE STOA OF ATTALOS

Ancient Agora site. Same hours as Agora (see box, p.29) but opens 11am on Mon. MAP P.28, POCKET MAP B12

For some background to the Agora, head for the **Stoa of Attalos**. Originally constructed around 158 BC, the Stoa was completely rebuilt between 1953 and 1956 and is, in every respect except colour, an entirely faithful reconstruction; with or without its original bright red and blue paint, it is undeniably spectacular.

A small **museum** occupies ten of the 21 shops that formed the lower level of the building. It displays items found at the Agora site from the earliest Neolithic occupation to Roman and Byzantine times. Many of the early items come from burials, but as ever the highlights are from the Classical era, including some good red-figure pottery and a bronze Spartan shield. Look out for the **ostraka**, or shards of pottery, with names written on them. At annual assemblies of the citizens, these *ostraka* would be handed in, and the individual with most votes banished, or "ostracized", from the city for ten years.

ILIAS LALAOUNIS MUSEUM

Kallispéri 12 ⓦ www.lalaounis-jewelry museum.gr. Wed 9am–9pm, Thurs–Sat 8.30am–4.30pm, Sun 11am–4pm. €5, free Wed after 3pm. MAP P.28, POCKET MAP C14

Greek jeweller **Ilias Lalaounis** forged an international reputation for his glamorous jewellery, once worn by Sixties icons like Liz Taylor and Jackie Kennedy, and still going strong today. In the 1950s, he spear-headed the revival of ancient Greek styles, drawing on inspiration from different eras from the Neolithic (items inspired by cave paintings) to Minoan, Cycladic and Mycenaean. He used ancient techniques, too, such as granulation and filigree.

Much of that early work, predominantly in gold, is on display in the **museum**, and it's absolutely gorgeous. There are also vast pieces of gold body jewellery, including snakes and octopuses that wrap themselves round the wearer. Upstairs is space for temporary exhibitions, while on the ground floor there's a small **workshop** where you can often watch a jeweller at work, as well as a shop selling jewellery and souvenirs – not all of which are outrageously expensive.

Shops

ACROPOLIS MUSEUM SHOP

Branches at the entrance to the Acropolis and at Garivâldi & Robérto Gálli, alongside Dionysos Zonar's. MAP P.28, POCKET MAP B13 & B14

Museum reproductions, posters and more; the two branches often seem to have completely different stock.

ALOGO

Hatzíkhristou 10. MAP P.28, POCKET MAP D8

An attractive souvenir shop selling handmade craft items, jewellery and art.

ELLINIKA KALOUDIA

Hatzíkhristou 8. MAP P.28, POCKET MAP D8

Cute little deli selling Greek wine and other edible souvenirs including honey and herbs.

NEWSSTAND

Athanasíou Dhiakoú 2. MAP P.28, POCKET MAP D14

A city-wide chain, but this branch of the newsagent specializes in international press, along with plenty of books in English, maps and guides.

STOA

Makriyiánni 5. MAP P.28, POCKET MAP D14

An arcade housing a number of interesting art and craft stores,

including tiny Trenotheatro, where there's inexpensive handmade jewellery and objects "inspired by the concept of train" – a real gem.

Cafés and restaurants

ACROPOLIS MUSEUM CAFÉ

Dhionysíou Areopayítou 15, in the Acropolis Museum. Tues–Sun 8am–8pm. MAP P.28, POCKET MAP C14

It's just as well that you can only get into this café if you've paid to get into the museum, as otherwise it would be permanently mobbed. There's a large internal area, plus a terrace looking up towards the Parthenon. Food is simple – salads, sandwiches, cakes – but of excellent quality, and prices are low (sandwiches €3, cappuccino €2.50). Try the delicious *píta me fakés*, a traditional lentil pie.

DIONYSOS ZONAR'S

Robérto Gálli 43 Ⓦ www.dionysoszonars.gr. Lunch & dinner daily. MAP P.28, POCKET MAP B14

This upmarket patisserie's unbeatable location opposite the Herodes Atticus Theatre is somewhat spoilt by being right above the main Acropolis coach park, and by the eye-watering prices. There's also a pricey restaurant.

OINOMAYIRIO TON THEON

Makriyiánni 23–27 ☎ 210 92 33 721, Ⓦ www.godsrestaurant.gr. Lunch & dinner daily. MAP P.28, POCKET MAP D14

The "Restaurant of the Gods" hardly lives up to its name, but it does serve decent taverna food at reasonable prices, very close to Akrópoli metro station. Set menus around €10–25; also open for breakfast.

Pláka

The largely pedestrianized area of Pláka, with its narrow lanes and stepped alleys climbing towards the Acropolis, is arguably the most attractive part of Athens, and certainly the most popular with visitors. In addition to a scattering of ancient sites and various offbeat and enjoyable museums, it offers glimpses of an older Athens, refreshingly at odds with the concrete blocks that characterize the rest of the metropolis.

Although surrounded by traffic-choked avenues, Pláka itself is a welcome escape, its narrow streets offering no through-routes for traffic. With scores of cafés and restaurants to fill the time between museums and sites, and streets lined with touristy shops, it's an enjoyable place to wander. The main disadvantage is price – things are noticeably more expensive here.

KYDHATHINÉON AND ADHRIANOÚ STREETS

An attractive approach to Pláka is to follow **Odhós Kydhathinéon**, a pedestrian walkway that starts near the Anglican and Russian churches on Odhós Filellínon. It leads gently downhill, past the Museum of Greek Folk Art, through café-crowded Platía Filomoússou Eterías,

TOURIST TRAFFIC IN PLÁKA

to **Odhós Adhrianoú**, which runs nearly the whole length of Pláka past the Roman Forum and interrupted by Hadrian's Library. These two are the main commercial and tourist streets of the district, with Adhrianoú increasingly tacky and downmarket as it approaches Platía Monastirakíou and the Monastiráki Flea Market.

JEWISH MUSEUM OF GREECE

Níkis 39 ⓦ www.jewishmuseum.gr. Mon–Fri 9am–2.30pm, Sun 10am–2pm. €5. MAP P.42-43, POCKET MAP E13

Elegantly presented and with plenty of explanation in English, the **Jewish Museum** tells the history of Jews in Greece. Downstairs are art and religious paraphernalia; the centrepiece is the **synagogue of Pátra**, dating from the 1920s, whose furnishings have been moved here en bloc and remounted.

Upstairs, more recent history includes World War II and the German occupation, when Greece's Jewish population was reduced from almost 80,000 to less than 10,000. There are features, too, on the part played by Jews in the Greek resistance, and stories of survival.

MUSEUM OF GREEK FOLK ART

Kydhathinéon 17 ⓦ www.melt.gr. Tues–Sun 9am–2pm. €2. MAP P.42-43, POCKET MAP D13

The **Folk Art Museum** is one of the most enjoyable in the city, despite being poorly lit and labelled. Its five floors are devoted to displays of weaving, pottery, costumes and embroidery, along with other traditional Greek arts and crafts. On the mezzanine floor, the carnival tradition of northern Greece and the all-but-vanished shadow-puppet theatre are featured.

The second floor features exhibits of jewellery and weaponry, much of it from the era of the War of Independence. The highlight, though, is on the first floor: the reconstructed room from a house on the island of Lesvós with a series of wonderful murals by the primitive artist **Theofilos** (1868–1934). These naive scenes are typical of the artist, who was barely recognized in his lifetime. Most of his career was spent painting tavernas and cafés on and around his native island, often paid only with food and board.

FRISSIRAS MUSEUM

Monís Asteríou 3 & 7 ⓦ www.frissiras museum.com. Wed–Fri 10am–5pm, Sat & Sun 11am–5pm. €3. MAP P.42-43, POCKET MAP D13

Housed in two beautifully renovated Neoclassical buildings, the **Frissiras Museum** is billed as Greece's only museum of **contemporary European art**, with over three thousand works – mostly figurative painting plus a few sculptures. The space at no. 7 houses the permanent exhibition, including plenty of names familiar to English-speakers – David Hockney, Peter Blake and Paula Rego among them – as well as many lesser-known European artists. Temporary exhibitions, along with a fine shop and an elegant café, are at no. 3, a block away.

GREEK CHILDREN'S ART MUSEUM

Kódhrou 9 ⓦ www.childrensartmuseum.gr. Tues–Sat 10am–2pm, Sun 11am–2pm; closed Aug. €2. MAP P.42-43, POCKET MAP D13

The **Children's Art Museum** holds a few permanent exhibits, but mainly the works are the winning entries to an annual nationwide art contest open to children up to the age of 14 – on the whole, it is a wonderfully uplifting place.

Pláka Ancient Agora

Stoa of Attalos (Agora Museum)

entrance

Hadrian's Library

Monument of Eponymous Heroes

Odeion of Agrippa

KLADHOU

DHEXIPPOU

ADHRIANOU

PLATIA AGORAS

KALOGIRONI

Forum Ticket Office

PIKILIS

PANS

Fethiye Mosque

Medresse

Museum of Greek Popular Musical Instruments

Palace & Stoas

EPAMINONDA

Roman Forum

Tower of the Winds

Turkish Baths

Ayii Apóstoli

POLYGNOTOU

THRASYVOULOU

LISSIOU

SHOPS

Amorgos	5
Eleftheroudakis	2
Elliniko Spiti	6
Finewine	9
Frissiras Museum Shop	8
Gorgona	4
Mesogaia	7
Museum of Musical Instruments Shop	1
Remember	3

Museum of Greek Folk Art: Man & Tools

Kanellopoulou Museum

Athens University Museum

ANAFIOTIKA

Ayios Nikólaos Ragavás

RESTAURANTS

Byzantino	15
Damingos (Ta Bakaliarakia)	18
Diogenes	19
Elaia	9
Fu-Rin-Ka-Zan	1
Mezedopolio Palio Tetradhio	8
Noodle bar	3
Palia Taverna Tou Psarra	10
Paradosiako	5
Platanos	4
Skholarhio	12
Yiasemi	7

Propylaia

Acropolis

Erechtheion

Boule Gate

Temple of Athena Nike

Parthenon

Monument of Thrasyllos

BAR

Brettos	17

Asklepion

Stoa of Eumenes

Theatre of Dionysos

Odeion of Pericles

CAFÉS

Amalthea	14
Café Pláka	11
Dhioskouri	6
Glykis	13
Ionos	16
Ydria	2

South Slope

LIVE MUSIC VENUES

Apanemia	2
Mostrou	1
Perivoli T'ouranou	3

AYÍA EKATERÍNI CHURCH

Platía Ayía Ekateríni. Mon–Fri 7.30am–12.30pm & 5–6.30pm, Sat & Sun 5–10pm. Free. MAP P.42–43, POCKET MAP D13

St Catherine's Church is one of the few in Pláka that's routinely open. At its heart is an eleventh-century Byzantine original – although this has been pretty well hidden by later additions. You can see it most clearly from the back of the church, while in the courtyard in front are foundations of a Roman building. Inside, the over-restored frescoes look brand new, and there are plenty of glittering icons.

AYIA EKATERINI CHURCH

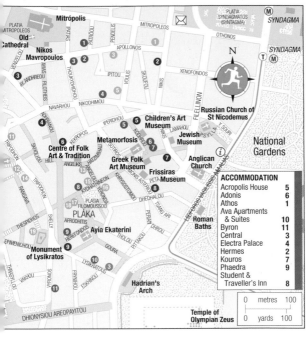

ACCOMMODATION

Acropolis House	5
Adonis	6
Athos	1
Ava Apartments & Suites	10
Byron	11
Central	3
Electra Palace	4
Hermes	2
Kouros	7
Phaedra	9
Student & Traveller's Inn	8

0	metres	100
0	yards	100

MONUMENT OF LYSIKRATOS

Platía Lysikrátous. MAP P.42–43, POCKET MAP D14

In the southeastern corner of Pláka, the **Monument of Lysikratos**, a graceful stone and marble structure from 335 BC, rises from a small, triangular open area overlooked by a quiet café-taverna. It's near the end of Odhós Tripódhon, a relic of the ancient Street of the Tripods, where winners of drama competitions erected monuments to dedicate their trophies, in the form of tripod cauldrons, to Dionysos. The Monument of Lysikratos is the only survivor of these triumphal memorials. A four-metre-high stone base supports six Corinthian columns rising up to a marble dome on which, in a flourish of acanthus-leaf carvings, the winning tripod was placed. The inscription tells us that

"Lysikratos of Kikyna, son of Lysitheides, was *choregos* [sponsor]; the tribe of Akamantis won the victory with a chorus of boys; Theon played the flute; Lysiades of Athens trained the chorus; Evainetos was *archon* [a senior public official]."

In the seventeenth century the monument became part of a **Capuchin convent**, which provided lodgings for European travellers – **Byron** is said to have written part of Childe Harold here, and the street beyond, Výronos, is named after him. The old Street of the Tripods, part of which has been excavated beside the monument, would have continued in this direction – many important ancient Athenian buildings are thought to lie undiscovered nearby.

CENTRE OF FOLK ART AND TRADITION

The **building** itself – designed for her in the 1920s in a Greek Art Nouveau or Arts & Crafts style – is a large part of the attraction, with its cool, high rooms and finely carved wooden doors, windows and staircase. At the back, narrow stairs descend to the kitchen with its original range, while upstairs there's a library and rooms where classes are held to pass on the traditions of crafts like embroidery and weaving.

ATHENS UNIVERSITY MUSEUM

Thólou 5 ⓦ www.history-museum.uoa.gr. Mon–Fri 9.30am–2.30pm, June–Sept also Mon & Wed 6–9pm. Free. MAP P.42–43, POCKET MAP D13

Occupying a fine old mansion, the site of Athens' first university, this museum has a wonderful collection of old **scientific and medical instruments** (labelled in Greek only). There are also scintillating views, especially from its top-floor terrace. While you're here, take a look to see if the **Kanellopoulou Museum**, nearby in the topmost house under the Acropolis at Théorias 12, has reopened after refurbishment. If so it's well worth a visit, with a lovely collection of antiquities.

CENTRE OF FOLK ART AND TRADITION

Angelikís Hatzimiháli 6. Tues–Fri 9am–1pm & 5–9pm, Sat & Sun 9am–1pm. Free. MAP P.42–43, POCKET MAP D13

The **Centre of Folk Art and Tradition** houses a collection of costumes, embroidery, lace and weaving, along with musical instruments, ceramics, and icons and religious artefacts. It occupies the former home of Angelikís Hatzimiháli, whose championing of traditional Greek arts and crafts was one of the chief catalysts for their revival in the early twentieth century.

MUSEUM OF GREEK FOLK ART: MAN AND TOOLS

Panós 22 ⓦ www.melt.gr. Tues–Sun 9am–2.30pm. €2. MAP P.42–43, POCKET MAP C13

The Anafiótika

Parts of Pláka, with stalls touting Manchester United beach towels and "Sex in Ancient Greece" playing cards, can become depressingly touristy. For a break, climb up into the jumble of streets and alleys that cling to the lower slopes of the Acropolis. Here, the whitewashed, island-style houses and ancient churches of the **Anafiótika** quarter proclaim a cheerfully architect-free zone. There's still the odd shop, and taverna tables are set out wherever a bit of flat ground can be found, but there are also plenty of hidden corners redolent of a quieter era.

A branch of the **Greek Folk Art Museum**, set in another fine mansion, this is devoted to the **world of work**. Tiny but fascinating and with good English labelling, its exhibits of tools and antiquated machinery concentrate on the pre-industrial world: there's a wooden grape-press as well as tools used in traditional trades including agriculture, barrel-making, cobbling and metalwork.

MUSEUM OF GREEK POPULAR MUSICAL INSTRUMENTS

Dhioyénous 1–3. Tues & Thurs–Sun 10am–2pm, Wed 12–6pm. Free. MAP P.42–43, POCKET MAP C12

Superbly displayed in the rooms of a Neoclassical building, the **Museum of Greek Popular Musical Instruments** traces the history of virtually every type of musical instrument that has ever been played in Greece. There are drums and wind instruments of all sorts (from crude bagpipes to clarinets) on the ground floor, lyras, fiddles, lutes and a profusion of stringed instruments upstairs. In the basement there are more percussion and toy instruments including some not-so-obvious festival and liturgical items such as triangles, strikers and livestock bells, along with carnival outfits. Reproductions of frescoes show the Byzantine antecedents of many instruments, and headphone sets are provided for sampling the music made by the various exhibits.

For the museum **shop**, see p.48.

TURKISH BATHS

Kiristou 8 ⓦ www.melt.gr. Mon & Wed–Sun 9am–2.30pm. €2. MAP P.42–43, POCKET MAP C13

Constructed originally in the 1450s, the **Turkish baths** were in use, with many later additions, right up to 1965. Newly restored (and sometimes called the Bath House of the Winds), they now offer an insight into a part of Athens' past that is rarely glimpsed and well worth a look.

Traditionally, the baths would have been used in shifts by men and women, although expansion in the nineteenth century provided the separate facilities you see today. The *tepidarium* and *caldarium*, fitted out in marble with domed roofs and rooflights, are particularly beautiful. The underfloor and wall heating systems have been exposed in places, while upstairs there are photos and pictures of old Athens. Labelling throughout is in Greek only, so it may be worth using the audio tour on offer (€1, plus deposit).

MUSEUM OF GREEK POPULAR MUSICAL INSTRUMENTS

Roman Athens

In 146 BC the Romans incorporated Athens into their vast new province of Achaia, whose capital was at Corinth. The city's historic status ensured that it was treated with respect, and Athenian artists and architects were much in demand in Rome, but Athens itself was a backwater.

The one Roman emperor who did spend a significant amount of time in Athens, and left his mark here, was **Hadrian** (reigned 117–138 AD). Among his grandiose monuments are Hadrian's Arch, a magnificent and immense library and (though it had been begun centuries before) the Temple of Olympian Zeus. A generation later, **Herodes Atticus**, a Roman senator who owned extensive lands in Marathon, became the city's last major benefactor of ancient times.

ROMAN FORUM

Entrance on Dhioskoúron. Daily: April–Sept 8am–7.30pm; Oct–March 8.30am–3pm. €2 or joint Acropolis ticket. MAP P.42–43, POCKET MAP C12

The **Roman Forum** was built during the reign of Julius Caesar and his successor Augustus as an extension of the older ancient Greek Agora. As today, its main entrance was on the west side, through the **Gate of Athena Archegetis**, which, along with the Tower of the Winds (see opposite), is still the most prominent remain on the site. This gate marked the end of a street leading up from the Greek Agora, and its four surviving columns give a vivid impression of the grandeur of the original portal.

On the opposite side of the Forum, part of which has now been built over, a second, less ostentatious gateway is also easily made out. Between the two is the **marketplace** itself, surrounded by colonnades and shops, some of which have been excavated. Inside the fenced site, but just outside the market area to the east, are the foundations of public latrines dating from the first century AD.

THE TOWER OF THE WINDS

Roman Forum. Same ticket.
MAP P.42–43, POCKET MAP C12

The best preserved and easily the most intriguing of the ruins inside the Forum site is the graceful octagonal structure

known as the **Tower of the Winds**. This predates the Forum, and stands just outside the main market area. Designed in the first century BC by Andronikos of Kyrrhos, a Syrian astronomer, it served as a compass, sundial, weather vane and water clock – the last powered by a stream from one of the Acropolis springs.

Each face of the tower is adorned with a relief of a figure floating through the air, personifying the eight winds. Beneath each of these it is still possible to make out the markings of eight sundials. The semicircular tower attached to the south face was the reservoir from which water was channelled into a cylinder in the main tower; the time was read by the water level viewed through the open northwest door. On the top of the building was a bronze weather vane in the form of the sea god, Triton. In Ottoman times, dervishes used the tower as a *tekke* or ceremonial hall, terrifying their superstitious Orthodox neighbours with their chanting, music and whirling meditation.

FETHIYE TZAMI

Roman Forum. MAP P.42–43, POCKET MAP C12

In the area around the Roman Forum can be seen some of the few visible reminders of the Ottoman city. The oldest mosque in Athens, the **Fethiye Tzami**, built in 1458, actually occupies a corner of the Forum site. It was dedicated by Sultan Mehmet II, who conquered Constantinople in 1453 (*fethiye* means "conquest" in Turkish). There's a fine, porticoed entrance, but sadly, you can't see inside, as it's now used as an archeological warehouse.

THE MEDRESSE

Corner of Eólou and Pelopídha.
MAP P.42–43, POCKET MAP C12

Just across the road from the Forum site, the gateway and single dome of a **medresse**, an Islamic school, survive. During the last years of Ottoman rule and the early years of Greek independence, this was used as a prison and was notorious for its bad conditions; a plane tree in the courtyard was used for hangings. The prison was closed in the 1900s and most of the building torn down.

Shops

AMORGOS

Kódhrou 3. MAP P.42–43, POCKET MAP D13

A small shop filled with an eclectic and varied collection of woodcarvings, needlework, lamps, lace, shadow puppets and more.

ELEFTHEROUDAKIS

Níkis 28. Mon–Fri 9am–9pm, Sat 9am–6pm. MAP P.42–43, POCKET MAP E12

This chain bookshop has a good selection of English-language books and maps.

ELLINIKO SPITI

Kekropós 14, just off Adhrianoú. MAP P.42–43, POCKET MAP D13

Amazing art and furniture created from found materials, especially driftwood but also metal and marble.

FINEWINE

Lysikrátous 3. MAP P.42–43, POCKET MAP D14

This tiny shop with a big variety of Greek and imported wines.

ELLINIKO SPITI

FRISSIRAS MUSEUM SHOP

Monís Asteríou 3. MAP P.42–43, POCKET MAP D13

Classy store selling posters, cards and upmarket gifts.

GORGONA

Adhrianoú 114. MAP P.42–43, POCKET MAP D13

Among the tourist traps of Adhrianoú, this has the feel of an older generation of souvenir shop, with sponges, puppet-theatre figures and cheap replica statues.

MESOGAIA

Níkis 52. MAP P.42–43, POCKET MAP E13

A very attractive deli with an excellent selection of oils, wines, honey and cheese.

MUSEUM OF MUSICAL INSTRUMENTS SHOP

Dhioyénous 1–3. MAP P.42–43, POCKET MAP C12

Excellent selection of CDs of traditional Greek music, plus some simple musical instruments.

REMEMBER

Adhrianoú 79. MAP P.42–43, POCKET MAP D12

Dimitris Tsouanato's shop has been around for over 25 years; if there is one piece of clothing you should buy in Athens it's one of his hand-painted T-shirts. Also stocks rock memorabilia and has some amazing sculptures in the courtyard.

Cafés

AMALTHEA

Tripódhon 16. MAP P.42–43, POCKET MAP D13

Tasteful if pricey café-patisserie, serving yoghurt and crêpes as well as non-alcoholic drinks.

CAFÉ PLÁKA

Tripódhon 1. MAP P.42–43, POCKET MAP D13

Touristy but convenient and elegantly refurbished – offers

tables of competing cafés: this is one of the best. A lovely place to sit outside for a quiet coffee or breakfast (they also serve more substantial meals), though, like its neighbours, very expensive.

Restaurants

BYZANTINO

Kydhathinéon 18, on Platía Filomoússou Eterías ☎ 210 32 27 368. Lunch & dinner daily. MAP P.42–43, POCKET MAP D13

Reliable, traditional taverna that still attracts locals on this touristy square. Take a look in the kitchen at the moderately priced daily specials, such as stuffed tomatoes, fish in lemon sauce or *youvétsi*.

crêpes, sandwiches, ice cream, wi-fi connections and a roof terrace on which to enjoy them.

DHIOSKOURI

Dhioskoúron, cnr Mitröon.
MAP P.42–43, POCKET MAP B13

Popular café right on the edge of Pláka overlooking the Agora. Simple food – salads and omelettes – as well as the inevitable frappés and cappuccinos.

GLYKIS

Angélou Yéronda 2. MAP P.42–43, POCKET MAP D13

A secluded corner under shaded trees just off busy Kydhathinéon, frequented by a young Greek crowd, with a mouthwatering array of sweets, as well as appetizer plates.

IONOS

Angélou Yéronda 7. MAP P.42–43, POCKET MAP D13

Good coffees and snacks, but above all a great place to people-watch on the busy Platía Filomoússou Eterías.

YDRIA

Adhrianoú 68, cnr Eólou.
MAP P.42–43, POCKET MAP C12

Platía Paliás Agorás, just round the corner from the Roman Forum, is packed with the

DAMINGOS (TA BAKALIARAKIA)

Kydhathinéon 41 ☎ 210 32 25 084, Ⓦ www .mpakaliarakia.gr. Dinner only; closed mid-July to end Aug. MAP P.42–43, POCKET MAP D13

Open since 1865 and tucked away in a basement, this place has dour service, but the old-fashioned style (hefty barrels in the back room filled with the family's home vintages, including a memorable retsina), and the excellent *bakaliáro skordhaliá* (deep-fried cod with garlic sauce) for which it is famed make up for it. Best in winter.

DIOGENES

Shelley 3, Platía Lysikrátous ☎ 210 32 24 845. Lunch & dinner daily. MAP P.42–43, POCKET MAP D13

Classy taverna and café with a delightfully shady, tranquil location overlooking the Monument of Lysikratos. Although the decor and clientele appear upmarket, prices aren't so different from anywhere else in Pláka: starters €5–9, mains like rabbit *stifado* or oven-baked lamb €10–15.

ELAIA

Erekhthéos 16 at Erotókritou ☎ 210 32 49
512. Mon–Sat dinner only, Sun noon–1am;
live music Thurs–Sat & Sun lunchtime.
MAP P.42–43, POCKET MAP C13

Modern taverna on three floors,
with wonderful views from
its roof terrace. The food is
Cretan-inspired and upmarket
(from €30 a head with house
wine), as is the decor, with
proper linen and glassware.

FU-RIN-KA-ZAN

Apóllonos 2 ☎ 210 32 29 170. Lunch &
dinner Mon–Fri, dinner only Sat & Sun.
MAP P.42–43, POCKET MAP D12

Busy Japanese restaurant –
popular at lunch – with sushi,
sashimi and yakisoba at reasonable prices. Other Japanese and
Asian restaurants are nearby.

MEZEDOPOLIO PALIO TETRADHIO

Mnisikléous 26, cnr Thrassívoulou
☎ 210 32 11 903. Lunch & dinner daily.
MAP P.42–43, POCKET MAP C13

One of the more touristy
tavernas with tables set out on
the stepped streets beneath the
Acropolis. The food is a cut
above the rest, though you pay
for the romantic setting. Live
music some evenings.

NOODLE BAR

Apóllonos 11 ☎ 210 33 18 585. Lunch &
dinner daily. MAP P.42–43, POCKET MAP D12

Fairly basic and inexpensive
place with plastic tables and a
roaring takeaway trade, serving
decent Asian food – Thai
predominantly but also with
Indian, Chinese and Indonesian
flavours. Part of a rapidly
growing chain.

PALIA TAVERNA TOU PSARRA

Erekhthéos 16 at Erotókritou ☎ 210 32 18 733,
🌐 www.psaras-taverna.gr. Lunch & dinner daily.
MAP P.42–43, POCKET MAP C13

The "Fisherman's Taverna" is a
large, classic Greek taverna set

PALIA TAVERNA TOU PSARRA

in a restored old mansion with
plenty of tables outside, on a
tree-shaded and bougainvillea-
draped pedestrian crossroads.
You're best making a meal of
the *mezédhes*, which include
humble standards as well as the
speciality seafood and fish
concoctions.

PARADOSIAKO

Voulís 44a ☎ 210 32 14 121. Lunch & dinner
daily. MAP P.42–43, POCKET MAP D12

Small place on a busy street
serving unpretentious,
reasonably priced, fresh Greek
food. Just three or four tables
on the pavement, and a similar
number inside.

PLATANOS

Dhioyénous 4 ☎ 210 32 20 666. Lunch &
dinner Mon–Sat. MAP P.42–43, POCKET MAP C12

A long-established taverna,
with outdoor summer seating
in a quiet square under the
plane tree from which it takes
its name. Good-value
traditional dishes such as
chops and roast lamb with
artichokes or spinach and
potatoes, and quaffable house
wine from vast barrels.

SKHOLARHIO

Tripódhon 14 ☎ 210 32 47 605,
Ⓦ www.sholarhio.gr. Daily 11am–2am.
MAP P.42–43, POCKET MAP D13

This attractive split-level taverna, known as *Kouklis* by the locals, has a perennially popular summer terrace, as well as great *mezédhes* (€2.50–5) displayed on trays so that you can point to the ones you fancy. Especially good are the flaming sausages, *bouréki* (pastry filled with ham and cheese) and grilled aubergine. The house red wine is also palatable and cheap. Deals for groups at around €14 a head.

YIASEMI

Mnisikléous 23 ☎ 210 32 18 929. Lunch & dinner daily. MAP P.42–43, POCKET MAP C13

A café-bistro on a steep, stepped street, *Yiasemi* offers a warm interior in winter for soup and hot chocolate, or tables outside for *meze* and inexpensive lunchtime specials, often vegetarian (such as stuffed baked potatoes for €5).

Bar

BRETTOS

Kydhathinéon 41. MAP P.42–43, POCKET MAP D13

By day a liquor store, selling mainly the products of their own family distillery, at night *Brettos* is one of the few bars in Pláka. It's a simple, unpretentious place with barrels along one wall and a huge range of bottles, backlit at night, along another.

Live music

APANEMIA

Thólou 4 ☎ 210 32 48 580.
MAP P.42–43, POCKET MAP C13

In the 1960s, *Apanemia* was at the forefront of the rediscovery of Greek music. Today, this backstreet "boite" is fashionable with a new generation, spearheading the new wave of acoustic Greek folk.

MOSTROU

Mnisikléous 22 ☎ 210 32 25 558. Daily from 11pm. MAP P.42–43, POCKET MAP C13

Big, taverna-style Greek music venue in the heart of Pláka. Things can get pretty rowdy when there's a local crowd in and the dancing starts. The cover charge (around €30) includes food.

PERIVOLI T'OURANOU

Lysikrátous 19 ☎ 210 32 35 517. Closed summer months. MAP P.42–43, POCKET MAP D14

Traditional rebétika club on the edge of Pláka (so used to tourists) with regular appearances by classy performer Babis Tsertsos. Entry varies, but even when free they make up for it on the food and drink – €15 for a beer, €25–30 for main-course dishes.

BRETTOS

Monastiráki and Psyrrí

Monastiráki and Psyrrí are enjoyable parts of Athens. Less touristy than Pláka to the south, there are nevertheless plenty of sights and extensive opportunities for eating, drinking and shopping. The Monastiráki area gets its name from the little monastery church on its central platía. Full of fruit stalls, nut sellers, lottery vendors and kiosks, the square lies at the heart of an area that has been a marketplace since Ottoman times and still preserves, in places, a bazaar atmosphere. Here the narrow lanes of Pláka start to open up, to streets that are noisier, busier and more geared to everyday living.

The traffic-free upper half of **Odhós Ermoú**, towards Sýndagma, is one of the city's prime **shopping** streets, full of familiar high-street chains and department stores: if you're after Zara or Marks & Spencer, Mothercare or Accessorize, this is the place to head. In the other direction, in the western half of the Flea Market (see p.56) and across Ermoú towards Psyrrí, are some funkier alternatives, with interesting new designer and retro stores mixed in with jumbley antiques places.

This is also a great place to **eat and drink**: between them, Monastiráki and Psyrrí probably have more restaurants and cafés per square metre than anywhere else in Athens. Monastiráki restaurants tend to be simple and functional – especially the line of tavernas that spill onto Mitropóleos as it heads up from Platía Monastirakíou. Psyrrí is more of a venue for an evening out – home to a throng of trendy restaurants, *mezedhopolía* and bars, buzzing till late every evening.

Psyrrí's own website – Ⓦ www.psirri.gr – is an excellent place to find out what's going on and lists virtually every restaurant, bar, shop and gallery in the area.

MONASTIRÁKI FLEA MARKET

MUSEUM OF GREEK FOLK ART: CERAMICS

Áreos 1 ⓦ www.melt.gr. Mon & Wed–Sun 9am–2.30pm. €2. MAP P.54–55, POCKET MAP C12

Squeezed between Hadrian's Library and the shacks of Pandhróssou stands the **Mosque of Tzisdarákis**. Built in 1759, it has had a chequered life – converted to a barracks and then a jail after Greek independence, before becoming the home of the **Greek Folk Art Museum** in 1918. Today, it houses the Kyriazópoulos collection of **ceramics** – the legacy of a Thessaloníki professor. Good as it is, the collection is likely to excite you only if you have a particular interest in pottery; most people will probably find the building itself, the only one of Athens' old mosques whose interior can be seen, at least as big an attraction.

Though missing its minaret, and with a balcony added inside for the museum, plenty of original features remain. In the airy, domed space, look out for the striped mihrab (the niche indicating the direction of Mecca), a calligraphic inscription above the entrance recording the mosque's founder and date, and a series of niches used as extra mihrabs for occasions when worshippers could not fit into the main hall.

HADRIAN'S LIBRARY

Entrance on Áreos. Daily 8.30am–3pm. €2 or joint Acropolis ticket. MAP P.54–55, POCKET MAP C12

Bordering the north end of the Roman Forum, and stretching right through from Áreos to Eólou, stand the surviving walls and columns of **Hadrian's Library**, an enormous building dating from 132 AD that enclosed a cloistered court of a hundred columns. Despite the name, this was much more than just a library – more a cultural centre, including art galleries, lecture halls and a great public space at its centre.

The site has only recently opened to the public and is still being excavated: much of it has been built over many times, and a lot of what you see today consists of the foundations and mosaic floors of later Byzantine churches. However, the entrance has been partly reconstructed, some of the original columns survive, and above all you get an excellent sense of the sheer scale of the original building (once entirely enclosed by walls and actually covering an area larger than the current site), especially when you realize that the Tetraconch Church, whose remains lie at the centre of the site, was built entirely within the library's internal courtyard.

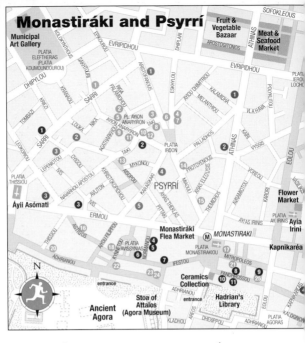

Map of Monastiráki and Psyrrí showing streets including Sofokleous, Evripidhou, Athinás, Ermoú, Adhrianoú; landmarks: Municipal Art Gallery, Fruit & Vegetable Bazaar, Meat & Seafood Market, Platía Eleftherías (Platía Koumoundoúrou), Platía Áyion Anaryíron, Platía Iróon, PSYRRÍ, Áyii Asómati, Flower Market, Ayía Iríni, Monastiráki Flea Market, Kapnikaréa, Ceramics Collection, Stoa of Attalos (Agora Museum), Ancient Agora, Hadrian's Library, Platía Monastirakíou.

THE IRIDHANÓS RIVER

Platía Monastirakíou. MAP P.54–55, POCKET MAP C12
The **Iridhanós** (or Eridanos) runs across Athens from its source on Lykavitós Hill, via Sýndagma and Monastiráki to Keramikós. Celebrated in Classical times, it had effectively been lost until the beginning of this century, when work on the metro expansion uncovered its underground course. Part of the ancient Greek and Roman system that turned it into an underground drain can be seen at Monastiráki metro station, and through railings and glass paving from the platía above. The brick vaulting of these ancient waterworks constitutes some impressive engineering work and in winter and spring, substantial amounts of water still course through.

THE KAPNIKARÉA

Ermoú, at Kapnikaréas. Mon, Wed & Sat 8am–1pm, Tues, Thurs & Fri 8am–12.30pm & 5–7.30pm, Sun 8–11.30am. Free.
MAP P.54–55, POCKET MAP C12

THE KAPNIKARÉA

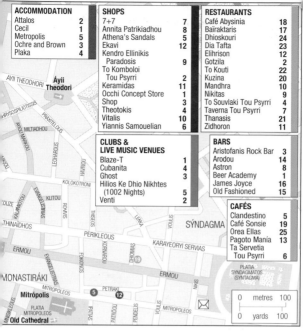

The pretty Byzantine church of **Kapnikaréa** marks more or less the beginning of the upmarket shopping on Ermoú, looking tiny in these high-rise urban surroundings. Originally eleventh century, but with later additions, it has a lovely little dome and a gloomy interior in which you can just about make out the modern frescoes. The church is allegedly named after its founder, a tax collector: *kapnós* means smoke, and in the Byzantine era a tax on houses was known as the smoke tax.

PLATÍA MITROPÓLEOS

MAP P.54–55, POCKET MAP D12

A welcome spot of calm among the busy shopping streets surrounding it, **Platía Mitropóleos** – Cathedral Square – is home to not just one but two cathedrals. The modern **Mitrópolis** is a large, clumsy nineteenth-century edifice; the **old cathedral** alongside it is dwarfed by comparison, but infinitely more attractive. There is said to have been a church on this site since the very earliest days of Christianity in Athens. What you see now dates from the twelfth century, a beautiful little structure cobbled together from plain and carved blocks from earlier incarnations – some almost certainly from that original church. There are several other small churches nearby: look out especially for the dusty, tiny chapel of Ayía Dhynámis, crouching surreally beneath the concrete piers of the Ministry of Education and Religion on Odhós Mitropóleos, a short way up the road towards Sýndagma.

Shops

7+7

Iféstou 22, in basement. MAP P.54–55, POCKET MAP B12

A choice selection of old and new rock and Greek music on vinyl and CD. The alley alongside has several other record and book stores, some very specialist, such as a store selling nothing but heavy metal LPs.

ANNITA PATRIKIADHOU

Pandhróssou 58. MAP P.54–55, POCKET MAP C12

Short on atmosphere, but genuine antiquities – pottery and coins mainly, some of them made into jewellery – are sold here, with official export licences to guarantee authenticity and legality. Prices are steep, but then many of the items are over 2000 years old.

ATHENA'S SANDALS

Normánou 7. Mon, Wed, Sat & Sun 10am–4pm, Tues, Thurs & Fri 10am–8pm. MAP P.54–55, POCKET MAP B12

Stavros Melissinos, the "poet sandal-maker", was an Athens institution, numbering The Beatles, Anthony Quinn and Sophia Loren amongst his hundreds of celebrity clients. Now retired, his daughter carries on his tradition here –

ATHENA'S SANDALS

Monastiráki Flea Market

In each direction from Platía Monastirakíou you'll see signs proclaiming that you are entering the famous **Monastiráki Flea Market**. These days this is a bit of a misnomer – there's plenty of shopping, but mostly of a very conventional nature. To the east, **Odhós Pandhróssou** is almost entirely geared towards tourists. West of Platía Monastiráki the flea market has more of its old character, and you'll find shops full of handmade musical instruments, or chess and *tavlí* boards, as well as places selling bikes, skateboards or camping gear. An alley off Iféstou is jammed with record and CD shops, with a huge basement secondhand bookshop. Around Normánou and Platía Avyssinías shops specialize in furniture and junky antiques: from here to Adhrianoú, the relics of the real flea market survive as hopeless jumble-sale rejects, touted by a cast of eccentrics (especially on Sundays). Odhós Adhrianoú is at its most appealing at this end, with a couple of interesting antique shops, and some shady cafés overlooking the metro lines, Agora and Akrópoli.

with interesting leatherwork of all kinds (belts, bags, slippers) alongside the sandals – while a son has a rival store nearby.

EKAVI

Mitropóleos 36. MAP P.54–55, POCKET MAP D12

"Games for adults", proclaims the sign outside. Not what you might think, but a huge variety of chess sets, roulette wheels and above all *tavlí* (backgammon) boards. Many are very reasonably priced.

KENDRO ELLINIKIS PARADOSIS

Entrances at Mitropóleos 59 and Pandhróssou 36. MAP P.54–55, POCKET MAP C12
As the name, "Centre of Hellenic Tradition", suggests, this pleasant upstairs emporium has a wide selection of traditional arts and crafts, especially ceramics and woodcarving, all at reasonable prices and with little of the hard sell often encountered in the nearby Flea Market. Even better is a selection of old Greek film posters and postcards.

KERAMIDAS

Pandhróssou 77. MAP P.54–55, POCKET MAP C12
Leather shop with an enormous selection of bags and purses in traditional Greek leather, better quality than most of its neighbours. Feel free to haggle over the price.

TO KOMBOLOI TOU PSYRRI

Ayíon Anaryíron 13. MAP P.54–55, POCKET MAP B11
A lovely little shop selling worry beads (komboloi) in every conceivable shape and size, plus handmade jewellery and crafts.

OCCHI CONCEPT STORE

Sarrí 35. MAP P.54–55, POCKET MAP A11
Occhi is a gallery/store based on the idea that clothing is art (or art can be worn); displaying the work of up-and-coming designers from around the world. Not just clothing – much of which is more wearable than it sounds – but jewellery, accessories and art too.

SHOP

Ermoú 112a. MAP P.54–55, POCKET MAP B11
Largest of a number of fashionable postmodern stores at the Psyrrí end of Ermoú, Shop deals in a wide range of designers and fashion labels, from Vivienne Westwood to Miss Sixty, as well as gifts, books, toys and music.

THEOTOKIS

Normánou 7. MAP P.54–55, POCKET MAP B12
One of a number of quirky antique/junk shops in this narrow street in the Flea Market. Prints, posters, postcards, old radios, typewriters, military uniforms: if you are looking for something specific it's amazing what they can find among their stock.

VITALIS

Pandhróssou 75. MAP P.54–55, POCKET MAP C12
Antiques, antiquities and curiosities including icons, old coins, glasswork and jewellery, as well as pieces of folk art. All in an environment that makes you feel as if you are discovering them for the first time.

YIANNIS SAMOUELIAN

Iféstou 36. MAP P.54–55, POCKET MAP B12
Long-established musical-instrument shop in the heart of the Monastiráki Flea Market, selling handmade guitars, lyras and the like.

Cafés

CAFÉ SONSIE

Dhiomías 2. MAP P.54–55, POCKET MAP D12

One of three adjacent café-bars, busy with weary shoppers and the after-work crowd, open long hours, every day. A good place to stop for coffee, just off the bustling Ermoú shopping strip, or for a late-night drink if you're staying nearby.

CLANDESTINO

Platía Ayíon Anaryíron. MAP P.54–55, POCKET MAP B11

It seems there's a café on every corner in Psyrrí, and this is one of the best. The building was once a *hamam*, hence the hubble-bubble pipes and floor cushions. Café by day and a chilled bar by night, with outdoor tables in summer.

OREA ELLAS

Mitropóleos 59 or Pandhróssou 36. Daily 9am–6pm. MAP P.54–55, POCKET MAP C12

Tucked away on the upper floor of the Kendro Ellinikis Paradosis store, this consciously old-fashioned *kafenío* offers a welcome escape from the crowded Flea Market for coffee, cakes and snacks. There's also a great view of the rooftops of Pláka.

PAGOTO MANÍA

Aisópou 21, cnr Táki. MAP P.54–55, POCKET MAP B11

Dozens of flavours of superb ice cream, as well as cakes, coffee and tea.

TA SERVETIA TOU PSYRRI

Eskhýlou 3. Open all day, through to the early hours. MAP P.54–55, POCKET MAP B11

A new place, but fabulously popular with locals for its traditional desserts and sticky cakes, washed down with tea, coffee or ouzo, according to taste.

Restaurants

CAFÉ ABYSINIA

Kynnétou 7, Platía Avyssinías.
☎ 210 32 17 047, ⓦ www.avissinia.gr.
Tues–Fri 10.30am–1am, Sat & Sun 10.30am–7pm. MAP P.54–55, POCKET MAP B12

With dining on two floors and a delicious, modern take on traditional Greek cooking (wild boar meatballs, moussaká with spinach or mussel pilaf), *Café Abysinia* is popular with a local alternative crowd. Though more expensive than many, it's good value, and there's live music most weekday evenings and weekend lunchtimes.

BAÏRAKTARIS

Mitropóleos 88, cnr Platía Monastirakíou
☎ 210 32 13 036. Lunch & dinner daily.
MAP P.54–55, POCKET MAP C12

Over a century old, this lively restaurant occupies two buildings, the walls lined with wine barrels and photos of celebrities. Some tables are on the pedestrian street, but the regulars eat in the cosy interior, where there's often impromptu, live traditional music. The inexpensive menu includes *souvláki*, *yíros* and oven dishes

CAFÉ ABYSINIA

BAIRAKTARIS

such as *tsoutsoukákia* (meatballs in tomato sauce).

DHIOSKOURI

Adhrianoú 37. ☏ 210 32 53 333. Lunch & dinner daily. MAP P.54–55, POCKET MAP B12

A very popular café-*mezedho-polío* with tables spreading across both sides of the pedestrianized street, some overlooking the metro lines. *Pikilía* – mixed meze plates – are good value at €10–17.

DIA TAFTA

Adhrianoú 37. ☏ 210 32 12 347. Lunch & dinner daily. MAP P.54–55, POCKET MAP B12

Near *Dhioskouri* (above), this café-*mezedhopolío* has tables out on the street but also a cavernous and inviting interior. Though you can just have a coffee or snack, served throughout the day, the emphasis here is more on the classic Greek food.

ELIHRISON

Ayíon Anaryíron 6 ☏ 210 32 15 220. Dinner Mon–Fri, lunch & dinner Sat & Sun. MAP P.54–55, POCKET MAP B11

Huge place at the heart of Psyrrí in a tastefully restored old building – lots of exposed stonework – with tables on several levels including a roof garden and spacious internal courtyard. Pricier than most, but classier too.

GOTZILA

Ríga Palamídhou 5 ☏ 210 32 21 086. Dinner only. MAP P.54–55, POCKET MAP B11

This good-value sushi bar in a quiet street off Platía Ayíon Anaryíron is mostly a late-night joint.

TO KOUTI

Adhrianoú 23 ☏ 210 32 13 229. Lunch & dinner daily. MAP P.54–55, POCKET MAP B12

Innovative Greek dishes as well as pasta and salads at this enjoyable, popular and slightly alternative restaurant. The menus are scrawled by hand in old children's books; the prices are slightly higher than average.

KUZINA

Adhrianoú 9 ☏ 210 32 40 133. ⓦ www.kuzina.gr. Lunch & dinner daily. MAP P.54–55, POCKET MAP B12

Far more adventurous than the average Greek taverna, *Kuzina*'s fusion cooking sets it well apart from its neighbouring rivals. Starters vary from staples like octopus to lamb spring rolls and crab cakes; mains (€17–20) also range from the traditional – lamb shanks with lemon sauce and wild herbs – to exotica like yellowfin tuna with ginger and wasabi or duck with green tea and figs.

MANDHRA

Ayíon Anaryíron 8, cnr Táki ☏ 210 32 18 387. Lunch & dinner daily. MAP P.54–55, POCKET MAP B11

Perennially popular choice at the heart of Psyrrí, with excellent live Greek music most evenings (not Mon & Tues) and standard taverna fare at prices that reflect the location.

NIKITAS

Ayíon Anaryíron 19 ☎ 210 32 52 591. Daily
11am–6pm. MAP P.54–55, POCKET MAP B11

A survivor from the days
before Psyrrí was fashionable,
and by far the cheapest option
here, with excellent home-
cooked taverna food and daily
specials, plus great chips.

TO SOUVLAKI TOU PSYRRI

Eskhýlou 14–16 ☎ 210 32 44 117. Daily
11am–2am. MAP P.54–55, POCKET MAP B11

Brightly-lit spot serving cheap
souvláki, grills and salads.

TAVERNA TOU PSYRRI

Eskhýlou 12 ☎ 210 32 14 923. Lunch &
dinner daily. MAP P.54–55, POCKET MAP B11

Some of the lowest prices and
tastiest food in Psyrrí. The
menu is an unusual take on
Greek classics, and is written in
deliberately obscure Greek, so
it may be easier to choose from
the kitchen.

THANASIS

Mitropóleos 69. Lunch & dinner daily.
MAP P.54–55, POCKET MAP C12

Reckoned to serve the best
souvláki and *yíros* in Psyrrí.
Inexpensive, and always packed
with locals at lunchtime: no
booking, so you'll have to fight
for a table. Watch out for the
side dish of peppers, which is
unusually fiery.

ZIDHORON

Táki 10, cnr Ayíon Anaryíron
☎ 210 32 15 368. Lunch & dinner daily;
closed Aug. MAP P.54–55, POCKET MAP B11

A typical Psyrrí upscale
mezedhopolío, in a great
location offering a vantage
point over the goings-on of the
area. It serves tasty Middle
Eastern foods like *pastourmás*,
halloumi and hummus, as well
as Greek favourites such as
baked feta, grilled peppers and
baked aubergine.

Bars

ARISTOFANIS ROCK BAR

Aristophánous 7, cnr Táki. From early
evening, daily. MAP P.54–55, POCKET MAP B11

A rock bar with a party
atmosphere and classic rock
sounds. Regular events such as
a Sunday "all the beer you can
drink in two hours for €10"
promotion.

ARODOU

Miaoúli, cnr Protoyénous.
MAP P.54–55, POCKET MAP B11

Miaoúli is packed with bars
and crowded with people every
evening. *Arodou* is right at the
heart – a big, busy place with
plenty of space both outside
and in. Not fancy, but a good
place to meet up before moving
on, and there's decent food too.

ASTRON

Táki 3 ☎ 697 74 69 356. Eves only, closed
Mon. MAP P.54–55, POCKET MAP B11

One of Psyrrí's busiest bars –
partly perhaps because it's so
small – which gets really
packed when the guest DJs
crank it up later on, playing
techno and minimal sounds.

ARODOU

BEER ACADEMY

Sarrí 18. MAP P.54–55, POCKET MAP B11
Big, three-storey branch of this
local chain with a huge choice
of beers from around the
world, plus solid, meaty Greek
food and grills to soak it up.

JAMES JOYCE

Ástigos 12 ☎ 210 32 35 055,
ⓦ www.jjoyceirishpubathens.com.
MAP P.54–55, POCKET MAP B11
Every city has to have its Irish
pub, but this central Athens
version was a late arrival. It was
worth waiting for – it's a really
friendly place with great
atmosphere, well-kept
Guinness (as well as any other
drink you might care to name),
Sky sports and regular live
acoustic music. There's also
very good pub-style food –
Irish breakfast, sausage and
mash, and steak and Guinness
pie, as well as Irish-style meze.

OLD FASHIONED

OLD FASHIONED

Miaoúli 16, cnr Thémidos. From 8pm daily.
MAP P.54–55, POCKET MAP C11
This small, quiet bar is a haven
of peace in this hectic area,
with just a few tables outside.
Attracts a slightly older crowd
than most around here.

Clubs and live music venues

BLAZE-T

Aristophánous 30 ☎ 210 32 34 823. Daily
11pm–4am. MAP P.54–55, POCKET MAP B10
Long-established by Psyrrí
standards, with sounds ranging
from hip-hop to techno.

CUBANITA

Karaïskáki 28 ☎ 210 33 14 605, ⓦ www
.cubanita.gr. MAP P.54–55, POCKET MAP B11
Enjoyable Cuban-themed bar/
restaurant/club, with plenty of
rum-based drinks, Cuban food
and Latin music, occasionally
live. Party atmosphere till the
early hours.

GHOST

Lepeniótou 26 ☎ 210 32 36 431.
MAP P.54–55, POCKET MAP B11
Live music venue in a huge
upstairs bar, mainly featuring
Greek rockers. The entry fee
(typically around €12) includes
your first drink.

HILIOS KE DHIO NIKHTES (1002 NIGHTS)

Karaïskáki 10, in the alley ☎ 210 33 17 293,
ⓦ www.1002nyxtes.gr. MAP P.54–55, POCKET MAP B11
Live music venue that's also a
bar and restaurant with a
Middle Eastern theme.
Arabic-inspired menus from
€25–50, plus traditional Greek
music which explores its
eastern roots – legendary Irish
lyra player Ross Daly is a
regular.

VENTI

Lepeniótou 20 ☎ 210 32 54 504, ⓦ www
.venti.gr. MAP P.54–55, POCKET MAP B11
Elegant, upmarket bar/club/
restaurant around a courtyard
with opening glass roof, with
dance music after midnight.

Thissío, Gázi and Áno Petrálona

Some of the most interesting and up-and-coming areas of Athens – Thissío, Gázi and neighbouring Roúf – lie to the west of the centre, where a new extension to Metro line 3, beyond Monastiráki, can only accelerate the pace of change. Nightlife and restaurants are the chief attractions here, but there's also a cluster of new museums and galleries, above all the Tekhnópolis centre and two annexes of the Benáki Museum, devoted to Islamic and modern art respectively.

Here too is **Kerameikos**, the chief burial ground of ancient Athens and a substantial section of the ancient city walls. South of Thissío, things are rather more traditional. Pedestrianized **Apóstolou Pávlou** leads around the edge of the Agora and Acropolis sites, under the flanks of the hills of the Pnyx and Filopáppou, and offers a pleasant, green escape from the city as well as fine views.

On the western side of the hills, the residential area of **Áno Petrálona** is a delight, entirely untouristy, with some excellent tavernas and a great open-air cinema, though absolutely nothing in the way of sights.

Between them, these places offer some excellent and authentic **eating and drinking** options – a welcome antidote to Pláka's tourist traps. You'll find everything from the lively, youth-oriented bars, clubs and restaurants of Gázi to sleepy, old-fashioned tavernas in Áno Petrálona. Thissío, easily accessible by metro, has some of the best evening and night-time views of the Acropolis from cafés around the traffic-free junction of Apóstolou Pávlou and Iraklidhón.

APÓSTOLOU PÁVLOU

MAP P.65, POCKET MAP A12–A13

You can follow pedestrianized **Odhós Apóstolou Pávlou** right around the edge of the Ancient Agora and Acropolis sites, from Metro Thissío to the Acropolis entrance. It's a rewarding walk, especially in the early evening, when the setting sun illuminates this side of the rock and the cafés of Thissío start to fill with an anticipatory buzz. Along the way, on either side, are all sort of minor remains of the ancient city.

SANCTUARY OF PAN

Off Apóstolou Pávlou. MAP P.65, POCKET MAP A13

As you follow Apóstolou Pávlou round there are a number of small excavations at the base of the hills. Perhaps the most interesting is the **Sanctuary of Pan**, on the lower slopes of the Pnyx just beyond the Thission open-air cinema. The cult of Pan was associated with caves, and in this fenced-off site you can see the opening to an underground chamber cut into the rock. Inside were found reliefs of Pan, a naked nymph, and a dog. There's also a mosaic floor

and, nearby, remains of an ancient road and two rock-cut, Classical-era houses.

FOUNTAIN OF PNYX

Off Apóstolou Pávlou. MAP P.65, POCKET MAP A14
Just above the Sanctuary of Pan is the so-called **Fountain of Pnyx**. In the sixth century BC a water system was engineered, with subterranean pipes bringing water from springs to cisterns that supplied the city. This is believed to be one of those: behind a locked entrance is a chamber with a Roman mosaic floor where the water was collected. You can also see traces of the concrete used to seal the chamber during World War II, when valuable antiquities were stored inside.

FILOPÁPPOU HILL

MAP P.65, POCKET MAP A14
From around the junction of Apóstolou Pávlou and Dhionysíou Areopayítou, below the Acropolis entrance, a network of paths leads up **Filopáppou Hill**, known in antiquity as the

"Hill of the Muses". Its pine- and cypress-clad slopes provide fabulous views of the Acropolis and the city beyond, especially at sunset (although night-time muggings have occurred here, so take care).

This strategic height has also played an important, if generally sorry, role in the city's history. In 1687 it was from here that the shell that destroyed the roof of the Parthenon was lobbed; more recently, the colonels placed tanks on the slopes during their coup of 1967. The hill's summit is capped by a grandiose monument to a Roman senator and consul, Filopappus, who is depicted driving his chariot on its frieze. To the west, paths lead across to Áno Petrálona through the ancient district of **Koile**. You can clearly see remnants of rock-cut houses here as well as the Koile road, which led from the city to the port at Pireás, protected by the Long Walls; a vital strategic thoroughfare in antiquity.

THE PRISON OF SOCRATES

Filopáppou Hill. MAP P.65, POCKET MAP A14

On the way up Filopáppou Hill, signed off to the left, is the so-called **Prison of Socrates**, in actual fact the rear part of a house – age unknown but probably very ancient – with rooms cut into the rock. The main structure would have been in front, and you can still see holes for joists and beams, and part of a rock-cut stairway.

ÁYIOS DHIMÍTRIOS

Filopáppou Hill. MAP P.65, POCKET MAP A14

The main path up Filopáppou Hill follows a line of truncated ancient walls past the attractive Byzantine church of **Áyios Dhimítrios**. The church is much venerated because, the story goes, its patron saint (St Dhimitrios "The Bomber") protected worshippers celebrating his saint's day here in 1656. The Turks planned to bombard the church, but instead "God sent a thunderbolt, exploding the powder and destroying their cannon, killing Yusuf Aga and his men". Inside, original Byzantine frescoes have been uncovered under later ones, the eyes of the saints gouged out.

THE PNYX

MAP P.65, POCKET MAP A13

In Classical times the **Hill of the Pnyx** was the meeting place of the democratic assembly, which gathered more than forty times a year. All except the most serious political issues were aired here, where a convenient semicircular terrace makes a natural spot from which to address the crowd. All male citizens could vote and, at least in theory, all could voice their opinions, though the assembly was harsh on inarticulate or foolish speakers.

There are some impressive remains of the original walls, which formed the theatre-like court, and of stoas where the assembly would have taken refreshment.

This atmospheric setting provides commanding Acropolis **views**, while benches on the west side allow you to contemplate the vista across Pireás and out to sea. On the northern slope, above Thissío, stands the impressive, Neoclassical bulk of the **National Observatory of Athens**.

THE HILL OF THE NYMPHS

MAP P.65, POCKET MAP B7

Over to the west a third hill rises – the **Hill of the Nymphs**. Nymphs were associated with the dusty whirlwinds to which this hill is particularly prone and it is said to be the location of the fairy sequences in Shakespeare's *A Midsummer Night's Dream*. Slightly lower and quieter than its better-known neighbours, this is a peaceful place with good views across to the western suburbs of Athens and beyond, as well as pleasant shaded walks.

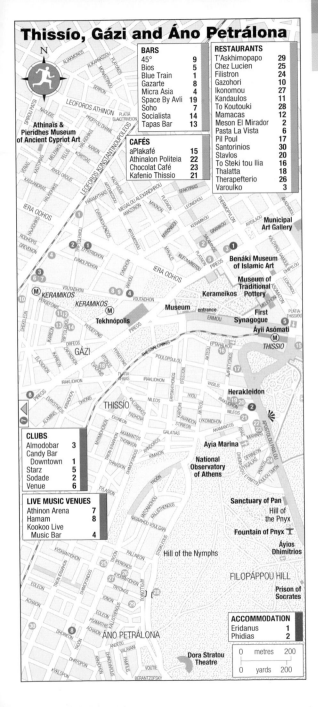

Thissío, Gázi and Áno Petrálona

N

BARS
45°	9
Bios	5
Blue Train	1
Gazarte	8
Micra Asia	4
Space By Avli	19
Soho	7
Socialista	14
Tapas Bar	13

CAFÉS
aPlakafé	15
Athinalon Politeia	22
Chocolat Café	23
Kafenio Thissio	21

RESTAURANTS
T'Askhimopapo	29
Chez Lucien	25
Filistron	24
Gazohori	10
Ikonomou	27
Kandaulos	11
To Koutouki	28
Mamacas	12
Meson El Mirador	2
Pasta La Vista	6
Pil Poul	17
Santorinios	30
Stavlos	20
To Steki tou Ilia	16
Thalatta	18
Therapefterio	26
Varoulko	3

Athinaïs & Pieridhes Museum of Ancient Cypriot Art

Municipal Art Gallery

Benáki Museum of Islamic Art

Museum of Traditional Kerameikos Pottery

KERAMIKOS

Tekhnópolis

First Synagogue

Áyii Asómati

THISSÍO

GÁZI

Herakleidon

THISSÍO

CLUBS
Almodobar	3
Candy Bar Downtown	1
Starz	5
Sodade	2
Venue	6

Ayia Marina

National Observatory of Athens

LIVE MUSIC VENUES
Athinon Arena	7
Hamam	8
Kookoo Live Music Bar	4

Sanctuary of Pan

Hill of the Pnyx

Fountain of Pnyx

Áyios Dhimitrios

Hill of the Nymphs

FILOPÁPPOU HILL

Prison of Socrates

ÁNO PETRÁLONA

ACCOMMODATION
Eridanus	1
Phidias	2

Dora Stratou Theatre

0	metres	200
0	yards	200

BENÁKI MUSEUM OF ISLAMIC ART

Áyion Asomáton 22, cnr Dhípylou Ⓦ www
.benaki.gr. Tues & Thurs–Sun 9am–3pm, Wed
9am–9pm. €5. MAP P.65, POCKET MAP A11

Antonis Benakis, founder of the **Benáki Museum** (see p.102), spent much of his life in Egypt, and this museum, in an elegantly converted Neoclassical mansion, was created to house the collection he amassed there. It follows a chronological course up through the building, from the seventh century on the first floor to the nineteenth on the fourth. Throughout there are beautiful, intricately decorated objects in almost every type of art: ceramics (especially tiles), metalwork and wood above all, but also textiles, jewellery, glass, scientific instruments, armour and more. The **highlights**, perhaps, are on the third floor, from the sixteenth- and seventeenth-century Golden Age of the Ottoman Empire under Suléyman the Magnificent. Here is a reconstructed room from a Cairo mansion, complete with inlaid marble floor, sunken fountains and elaborate wooden window-screens, as well as silk wall-hangings (not from the mansion), shot with silver and gold thread.

There's a top-floor **café** overlooking the Kerameikos site with industrial Gázi beyond, as well as views of the Acropolis and Filopáppou, while in the basement stands a substantial chunk of the ancient city wall, almost 6m high, that was preserved during the building's restoration.

KERAMEIKOS

Entrance on Ermoú. Daily: April–Sept
8am–7.30pm; Oct–March 8.30am–3pm;
museum opens 11am Mon. €2 or joint
Acropolis ticket. MAP P.65, POCKET MAP B5

The **Kerameikos** (or Kerameikós) site, encompassing one of the principal burial grounds of ancient Athens and a hefty section of the ancient wall, provides a fascinating and quiet retreat. Little visited, it has something of an oasis feel, with the lush Iridhanós channel (see p.54), speckled with water lilies, flowing across the site from east to west.

To the right of the entrance is the stream and the double line of the city wall. Two roads pierced the wall here, and the gates that marked their entrance to the city have been excavated: the great **Dipylon Gate** was the busiest in the ancient city, where the road

KERAMEIKOS

from Pireás, Eleusis and the north arrived; the **Sacred Gate** was a ceremonial entrance where the Ierá Odhós or Sacred Way entered the city – it was used for the Eleusinian and Panathenaic processions (see p.30 & p.124).

Branching off to the left from the Sacred Way is the **Street of the Tombs**, the old road to Pireás. In ancient Greece people were frequently buried alongside roads, a practice at least partly related to the idea of death as a journey. This site was clearly a prestigious one and numerous commemorative monuments to wealthy or distinguished Athenians have been excavated, their original stones reinstated or replaced by replicas. The flat, vertical stelae were the main funerary monuments of the Classical world; the sarcophagi that you see are later, from Hellenistic or Roman times. The large tomb with the massive semicircular base to the left of the path is the **Memorial of Dexileos**, the 20-year-old son of Lysanias of Thorikos, who was killed in action at Corinth in 394 BC. The adjacent plot contains the **Monument of Dionysios** of Kollytos, in the shape of a pillar stele supporting a bull carved from Pentelic marble.

The site **museum** is a lovely, cool, marble-floored space displaying finds from the site and related material, above all stelae and grave markers. There are also many poignant funerary offerings – toys from child burials, gold jewellery and beautiful small objects of all sorts. The ceramics are particularly fine, including lovely dishes with horses on their lids (*pyxides*) from the early eighth century BC and some stunning fifth-century-BC black-and-red figure pottery.

TEKHNÓPOLIS

TEKHNÓPOLIS

Pireás 100 ☎ 210 34 67 322, Ⓦ www .cityofathens.gr. Daily 10am–10pm.
MAP P.65, POCKET MAP B5

The former gasworks from which the Gázi district takes its name has been converted into a stunning series of spaces for concerts and changing exhibitions, mostly of **contemporary art and photography**. Two round gas-holders have become circular glass offices – one for Athens 98.4FM, the other for Tekhnópolis administration – while in the various pumping stations and boiler rooms surrounding them, galleries and exhibition halls of varying sizes, as well as a café, have been created, many with parts of the original machinery preserved. The **Maria Callas Museum** that used to be here is in the process of being moved (to another site within the complex), but all sorts of temporary exhibitions and concerts take place here so it's well worth taking a look – or check local listings magazines for details.

TRADITIONAL POTTERY MUSEUM

Melidhóni 4. Mon–Fri 9am–3pm, Sun 10am–2pm. €3. MAP P.65, POCKET MAP A11

The tiny **Traditional Pottery Museum** has exhibits on pottery-making methods, with regular hands-on demonstrations. A couple of further galleries have temporary exhibits, usually on a particular style or era of pottery. There's also a small café and a shop selling quality ceramics.

BENÁKI MUSEUM PIREÓS STREET ANNEXE

Pireós 138, cnr Andhrónikou Ⓦ www.benaki .gr. Wed, Thurs, Sun 10am–6pm, Fri & Sat 10am–10pm. Exhibition prices vary. Metro Petrálona, or many buses along Pireós including #049, #914 & trolley bus #021. POCKET MAP A6

Six blocks southwest of Tekhnópolis, the new **Benáki cultural centre** is symptomatic of the development that is transforming a formerly industrial part of the city. There's no permanent collection, but the prestige of the Benáki Museum attracts exceptional temporary shows so it's worth checking what's on. The vast industrial space, now clad in pink marble, has been converted to galleries around an internal courtyard, and there's an airy, upmarket **café/restaurant** too.

ATHINAÏS

Kastoriás 34–36 Ⓦ www.athinais.com.gr. MAP P.65, POCKET MAP A4

A magnificent restoration of an early twentieth-century silk factory, the **Athinaïs complex** contains a theatre, music space, movie screen, two restaurants, a bar and café, exhibition halls, a museum (temporarily closed) and, the real purpose of the place, a sizeable conference centre. The museum shop (still open) is full of lavish – and lavishly priced – arty gifts, while upstairs are galleries with temporary exhibitions. Details of what's on can be found on the website or in the local press.

HERAKLEIDON

Iraklidhón 16 Ⓦ www.herakleidon-art.gr. Tues–Sat 1–9pm, Sun 11am–7pm. €6. MAP P.65, POCKET MAP A12

Describing itself as an Experience in Visual Arts, the small **Herakleidon gallery** has a rota of temporary exhibitions, usually excellent and often featuring works from the permanent collection, which includes one of the world's biggest collections of M.C. Escher, as well as Hungarian/French artist Victor Vasarely, a leader of the Op Art movement, and Toulouse-Lautrec.

Cafés

APLAKAFÉ

Adhrianoú 1. MAP P.65, POCKET MAP A12
Right by Platía Thissíou, this
large café is a popular place to
meet up, with tables outside
as well as in a courtyard that's
covered in winter. Breakfasts,
sandwiches, pizzas and burgers
served (€3–7) as well as the
ubiquitous coffees and frappés.
By night, there's music and
more of a bar atmosphere.

ATHINAION POLITEIA

Akamántos 1, cnr Apóstolou Pávlou.
MAP P.65, POCKET MAP A12
An enviable position in an
old mansion, with great views
from the terrace towards
the Acropolis, makes this an
excellent place to relax over a
frappé. Light meals also served.

CHOCOLAT CAFÉ

Apostólou Pávlou 27. MAP P.65, POCKET MAP A12
Another café with a fabulous
Acropolis view from its
outdoor tables, *Chocolat* is an
exceptionally glitzy affair with
tables indoors on a number
of levels leading up to a
spectacular roof terrace. Open
all day for pricey breakfasts
and coffees – €8 for a smoothie,
club sandwich €12–16 – and
a glamorous setting in the
evening for cocktails. Next
door is a branch of the *Flocafé*
chain with rather more
ordinary prices.

KAFENIO THISSIO

Akamántos 2. MAP P.65, POCKET MAP A12
Slightly cheaper than the cafés
with the views (though still
€4 for a sandwich, €6 for an
omelette), this place has a
slightly alternative atmosphere
– a change from the sometimes
intimidating slickness of many
of Thissío's cafés.

Restaurants

T'ASKHIMOPAPO

Iónon 61 ☎ 210 34 63 282. Lunch & dinner
daily; closed Sun & mid-May to mid-Sept.
MAP P.65, POCKET MAP B8
The "Ugly Duckling" is a
wonderful winter-only taverna
with *mezédhes* and unusual
mains. Occasional live music,
and a rooftop for balmy days.

CHEZ LUCIEN

CHEZ LUCIEN

Tróön 32 ☎ 210 34 64 236. Dinner Tues–Sat.
MAP P.65, POCKET MAP A7
Excellent French bistro with a
short menu of authentic, well-
prepared dishes at reasonable
prices; you may have to share
a table. No booking, and when
it's busy (most of the time)
there are two sittings, at 8pm &
10.30pm.

FILISTRON

Apóstolou Pávlou 23 ☎ 210 34 22 897,
ⓦ www.filistron.com. Tues–Sun noon–midnight.
MAP P.65, POCKET MAP A13
Touristy, but worth it for the
roof terrace with Acropolis
view. Short menu of tasty
mezédhes from all over Greece,
which means some interesting
and unusual dishes; good value
given the location.

IKONOMOU

GAZOHORI

Dhekeléon 1 & 5 ☎ 210 34 24 044. Lunch & dinner daily. MAP P.65, POCKET MAP A5

A big, busy place in two separate buildings, attracting a typically young Gázi crowd. Traditional meze served on marble-topped tables at reasonable prices; large *pikilía* (meze selection) €16.

IKONOMOU

Tróön 41, cnr Kydhantídhon ☎ 210 34 67 555. Lunch & dinner Mon–Sat. MAP P.65, POCKET MAP A7

This wonderful traditional taverna serves up home-cooked food to packed pavement tables in summer. There's no menu, just a dozen or so inexpensive daily specials: check out what others are eating as the waiters may not know the names of some of the dishes in English.

KANDAULOS

Persefónis 49 ☎ 210 34 24 725. Lunch & dinner daily. MAP P.65, POCKET MAP A5

High-class, bustling *psistariá* for grilled meat, *souvláki* and *yíros*. Busy for takeaway but also plenty of tables.

TO KOUTOUKI

Lakíou 9 (reached from Filopáppou Hill, or by a tunnel under the main road) ☎ 210 34 53 655. Lunch & dinner Mon–Sat. MAP P.65, POCKET MAP B7

Inexpensive, traditional taverna with good *fáva* and grilled meat. Pleasantly rural atmosphere despite the proximity of the flyover, with no houses nearby and roof seating overlooking Filopáppou Hill.

MAMACAS

Persefónis 41 ☎ 210 34 64 984. Lunch & dinner daily. MAP P.65, POCKET MAP A5

One of the restaurants that made Gázi fashionable, and still a favourite with the young, stylish and well-heeled. The white decor spreads through a house and across several terraces. Service can be slow, but the food – traditional Greek, *mezédhes*-style, with a modern twist – is reliably good. It's fairly pricey and, like everywhere here, doesn't get lively till late; some time after midnight, the DJs take over. Booking advised.

MESON EL MIRADOR

Ayisiláou 88, cnr Salamínos ☎ 210 34 20 007. Lunch & dinner Mon–Sat. MAP P.65, POCKET MAP B5

MAMACAS

Authentic Mexican restaurant in an elegant restored mansion in Keramikós, with tables on a lovely roof terrace. Gets enjoyably rowdy later on.

PASTA LA VISTA

Voutádhon 58, cnr Dhekeléon ☎ 210 34 61 932, ⓦ www.pastalavista.gr. Lunch & dinner daily. MAP P.65, POCKET MAP A5

If you're after something simple to eat in Gázi, head here for pizza and pasta at prices ranging from €7 to €14.

PIL POUL

Apostólou Pávlou 51, cnr Poulopoúlou ☎ 210 34 23 665. Lunch & dinner Tues–Sun. MAP P.65, POCKET MAP A12

Fancy and expensive modern French/Mediterranean restaurant; there's a tasting menu for €60. The food is occasionally over-elaborate, but the roof terrace in this 1920s mansion offers immaculate Acropolis views in an incomparably romantic setting. There's a chilled-out bar/club (also *Pil Poul*) downstairs in the same building. Booking essential.

SANTORINIOS

Dhoriéon 8 ☎ 210 34 51 629. Lunch & dinner daily. MAP P.65, POCKET MAP A8

Unpretentious, inexpensive "wine-taverna" whose main decoration is provided by vast barrels of Santorini wine. Swill it down with good *mezédhes* in the whitewashed courtyard.

STAVLOS

Iraklidhón 10 ☎ 210 34 67 206, ⓦ www.stavlos.gr. Dinner Mon–Thurs, lunch & dinner Fri–Sun. MAP P.65, POCKET MAP A12

Originally used as royal stables during the nineteenth century, *Stavlos* is now a hugely popular meeting point, with numerous seating areas including a large internal courtyard. Italian-influenced restaurant, as well as a bar, gallery and club.

TO STEKI TOU ILIA

Eptahálkou 5 ☎ 210 34 58 052. Dinner Tues–Fri, lunch & dinner Sat & Sun. MAP P.65, POCKET MAP A12

This simple, cheap place on a pedestrianized street above the metro tracks is so popular that the owners have opened a second branch 200m further down the road (at Thessaloníkis 7). It's renowned for some of the finest lamb chops in the city, and has tables out on the street in summer.

THALATTA

Vítonos 5 ☎ 210 34 64 204. Dinner Mon–Sat. MAP P.65, POCKET MAP A6

A lovely, upmarket seafood restaurant with marine decor (*thalatta* means "sea" in the Athenian dialect of Ancient Greek), in a thoroughly unprepossessing location. Specialities include oysters, in season, and whole fresh fish baked in salt. There's an internal courtyard in summer. €50 or more a head if you push the boat out.

THERAPEFTERIO

Kydhantidhón 41 ☎ 210 34 12 538. Lunch & dinner daily. MAP P.65, POCKET MAP A7

The largest of a number of traditional tavernas near *Ikonomou* (see opposite), also with pavement tables and excellent, inexpensive Greek dishes.

VAROULKO

Pireós 80 ☎ 210 52 28 400, ⓦ www.varoulko.gr. Dinner Mon–Sat. MAP P.65, POCKET MAP A10

Chef Lefteris Lazarou earned a Michelin star for his restaurant in Pireás; now downtown, the prices reflect that (€80 or more a head). When they come off, though, the elaborate and innovative seafood dishes are worth it: the cool, modern setting includes a summer roof terrace with Acropolis views. Booking essential.

Bars

45°

Íakhou 18, cnr Voutádhon ☎ 210 34 72 729.
Opens around 9pm; closed Mon. MAP P.65,
POCKET MAP A5

A big, lively, rock-music-based
bar-club, one of the longest-
established places in Gázi.
Opens relatively early and
there's a rooftop terrace with
Acropolis views.

BIOS

Pireós 84 ☎ 210 34 25 335, ⓦ www.bios.gr.
MAP P.65, POCKET MAP B5

Boho art-space/café/bar/club
with frequent happenings of
performance art or experi-
mental theatre. There's
something going on most
evenings, and a late-night
basement dance-space with
avant-garde sounds.

BLUE TRAIN

Konstantinoupóleos 84 ☎ 693 21 01 127.
MAP P.65, POCKET MAP A4

With a courtyard in summer,
and open from early evening,
this is a popular gay meeting-
place before going on to the
clubs. Upstairs, *Kazarma* (same
phone) is one of the better
clubs you could go on to, while
El Cielo, higher still, is a
summer roof-terrace bar.

GAZARTE

Voutádhon 32 ☎ 210 34 60 347.
ⓦ www.gazarte.gr. MAP P.65, POCKET MAP A5

Bar, café, shop and arty space,
including a roof terrace. You can
just stop by for a coffee or beer,
but there are all sorts of events
here too, including live jazz and
world music.

MICRA ASIA

Konstantinoupóleos 70 ☎ 210 34 64 851.
MAP P.65, POCKET MAP A5

Old house converted to a bar
on several floors, including
roof space. The name means
Asia Minor, and there's an
Ottoman theme, with chilled
music to match. Occasional
exhibitions, and DJs at
weekends, often with a world
music emphasis.

SPACE BY AVLI

Iraklidhón 14. MAP P.65, POCKET MAP A12

In the heart of the Thissío bar
area, this daytime café-bar
evolves at night into a funky
club with jazz and soul sounds.

SOHO

Voutádhon 54 ☎ 210 34 22 663.
MAP P.65, POCKET MAP A5

There's a row of half a dozen bar/
clubs at the top of Voutádhon,
with dance music and a youthful

crowd. *Soho* is the biggest and arguably the best of them. In the early evening there are tables outside and it's a calm meeting place; later on, the action moves to the DJs inside.

SOCIALISTA

Triptolémou 33 ☎ 210 34 74 733.
MAP P.65, POCKET MAP A5

Big, enjoyable bar/club in the midst of the action in Gázi, with Latin sounds and occasional live music.

TAPAS BAR

Triptolémou 44 ☎ 210 34 71 844. Eves only, closed Sun. MAP P.65, POCKET MAP A5

Despite the name you won't find many people eating the tapas here, but it's busy and buzzy till the early hours – handy for the Gázi clubs – with good cocktails and a pleasant outdoor space.

Clubs

ALMODOBAR

Konstantinoupóleos 60 ☎ 694 64 57 442, Ⓦ www.myspace.com/almodobar. MAP P.65, POCKET MAP A5

Intimate club with techno and deep house sounds, plus occasional forays into live acts and electro jazz.

CANDY BAR DOWNTOWN

Ierá Odhós 41 ☎ 210 34 63 080. €15 entry.
MAP P.65, POCKET MAP A5

Huge club that draws a big out-of-town crowd with wild theme-nights and visiting DJs. There's a party atmosphere, and club, house and R&B on the decks.

SODADE

Triptolémou 10 ☎ 210 34 68 657.
MAP P.65, POCKET MAP A5

Stylish gay and lesbian crowd and great music – one room

plays Greek and mainstream, the other quality dance music.

STARZ

Asomáton 1, Platía Thissíou ☎ 210 32 24 553.
Fri–Sun only. MAP P.65, POCKET MAP A11

Big, mainstream club with DJ guest nights and a young crowd. They also stage concerts featuring Greek pop stars.

VENUE

Pireós 130, Roúf ☎ 210 34 11 410, Ⓦ www.venue-club.com. Fri & Sat only.
€15 entry. MAP P.65, POCKET MAP A6

Venue is one of Athens' biggest clubs, with three separate dance floors. Legendary local house DJ Vassilis Tsilichristos features most Saturdays, and there's a roster of top international names to supplement him.

Live music

ATHINON ARENA

Pireós 166, Roúf ☎ 210 34 71 111.
MAP P.65, POCKET MAP A7

The Athens Arena is a huge concert hall in an up-and-coming industrial area just down from Gázi. Stages a variety of events, but above all *bouzoúkia* (glitzy modern Greek music) with local stars like Anna Vissi.

HAMAM

Dhimofóndos 97 ☎ 210 34 21 212.
Entry around €15, including first drink.
MAP P.65, POCKET MAP A8

Traditional Greek music in a former Turkish *hamam* in Áno Petrálona.

KOOKOO LIVE MUSIC BAR

Iákhou 17 ☎ 210 34 50 930, Ⓦ www.kookoo .gr. Entry typically €12, including a drink.
MAP P.65, POCKET MAP B5

Fun new live music venue, featuring young Greek alternative and rock musicians.

Sýndagma and around

All roads lead to Sýndagma – you'll almost inevitably find yourself here sooner or later for the metro and bus connections. Platía Syndágmatos, or Constitution Square, to give it its full name, lies roughly midway between the Acropolis and Lykavitós Hill. With the Greek Parliament building (the Voulí) on its uphill side, and banks, offices and embassies clustered around, it's the political and geographic heart of Athens.

The square's name derives from the fact that Greece's first constitution was proclaimed by King Otto from the palace balcony in 1843. It's still the principal venue for mass demonstrations, and in the run-up to elections the major political parties stage their final campaign rallies here.

Vital hub as it is, however, the traffic and the crush ensure it's not an attractive place to hang around. Escape comes in the form of the **National Gardens**, a welcome area of greenery stretching out south from the parliament building and offering a traffic-free route down past the **Záppio** to **Hadrian's Arch** and the **Temple of Olympian Zeus**, or across to the Panathenaic Stadium (p.110). In other directions Odhós Ermoú, prime shopping territory, heads west towards Monastiráki, with Pláka and the Acropolis to the southwest; Stadhíou and Panepistimíou head northwest towards Omonía; while to the north and east lie Kolonáki and the embassy quarter.

THE VOULÍ

Platía Syndágmatos. MAP P.75, POCKET MAP F12
The Greek National Parliament, the **Voulí** (not open to the public), presides over Platía Syndágmatos from its uphill (east) side. A vast, ochre-and-white Neoclassical structure, it was built as the royal palace for Greece's first monarch, the Bavarian King Otto, who moved in in 1842. In front of it, goose-stepping *evzónes* in tasselled caps, kilts and woolly leggings – a prettified version of traditional mountain costume – change their guard at intervals in front of the **Tomb of the Unknown Soldier**. On Sundays, just before 11am, a full band and the entire corps parade from the tomb to their barracks at the back of the National Gardens to the rhythm of innumerable camera shutters.

THE VOULÍ

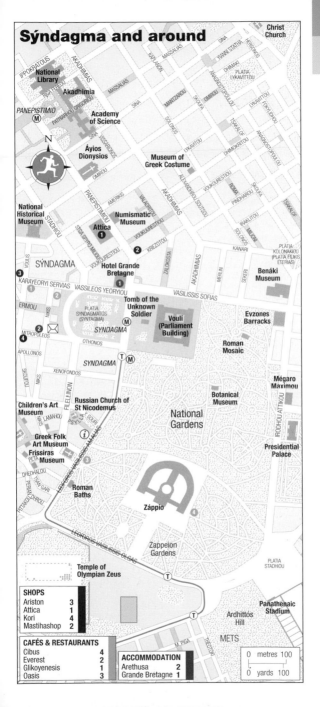

Sýndagma and around

SHOPS

Ariston	3
Attica	1
Kori	4
Mastihashop	2

CAFÉS & RESTAURANTS

Cibus	4
Everest	2
Glikoyenesis	1
Oasis	3

ACCOMMODATION

| Arethusa | 2 |
| Grande Bretagne | 1 |

HOTEL GRANDE BRETAGNE

Vasiléos Yeoryíou 1 ☎ 210 33 30 000, Ⓦ www.grandebretagne.gr. MAP P.75, POCKET MAP E12

With the exception of the Voulí, the vast **Hotel Grande Bretagne** – Athens' grandest – is just about the only building on Sýndagma to have survived postwar development. Past the impressive facade and uniformed doormen, the **interior** is magnificently opulent, as befits a grand hotel established in the late nineteenth century. It's worth taking a look inside, or having a drink at one of the bars: the rooftop pool, bar and restaurant boast great views across the city.

The hotel has long been at the centre of Greek political intrigue: in one notorious episode, **Winston Churchill** narrowly avoided being blown up here on Christmas Day 1944, when saboteurs from the Communist-led ELAS resistance movement placed an enormous explosive charge in the drains. According to whom you believe, the bomb was either discovered in time by a kitchen employee, or removed by ELAS themselves when they realized that Churchill was one of their potential victims.

THE NATIONAL GARDENS

Entrances on Amalías, Vasilíssis Sofías and Iródhou Attikoú. Daily sunrise–sunset. Free. MAP P.75, POCKET MAP E12–F14

The most refreshing acres in the city are the **National Gardens** – not so much a flower garden as a luxuriant tangle of trees, whose shade and duck ponds provide palpable relief from the heat in summer. The gardens were originally the private palace gardens, a pet project of Queen Amalia in the 1840s; supposedly the main duty of the tiny Greek navy in its early days was to fetch rare plants, often the gifts of other royal houses, from remote corners of the globe. Despite a major pre-Olympics clear-out, there's still something of an air of benign neglect here, with rampant undergrowth and signs that seem to take you round in circles.

It's a great place for a picnic, though, or just a shady respite from the city streets. There are benches everywhere, ducks being fed in the ponds, and other attractions including a zoo, a children's playground (on the Záppio side) and a botanical museum. The tiny **zoo** has wild goats and some exotic fowl, but most

CHESS-PLAYERS IN THE ZÁPPIO

of the cages these days are occupied by chickens, rabbits and domestic cats. The **Botanical Museum** (closed for refurbishment at the time of writing) occupies an elegant little pavilion nearby. As everywhere in Athens, there are also archeological remains everywhere, and here they seem particularly neglected and unloved. Look out, for example, for the large, barely labelled **Roman mosaic** at the back of the Voulí, near the Vasilíssis Sofías entrance.

HADRIAN'S ARCH

THE PRESIDENTIAL PALACE

Iródhou Attikoú, cnr Vasiléos Yeoryíou B. MAP P.75, POCKET MAP G7

Across the road from the far side of the gardens is the **Presidential Palace**, the royal residence until Constantine's exile in 1967, where more *evzónes* stand on sentry duty. Next door, the slightly more modest **Mégaro Maxímou** is the official residence of the prime minister.

THE ZÁPPIO

Open 24hr. MAP P.75, POCKET MAP F13

On the southern side of the National Gardens are the graceful, crescent-shaped grounds of the **Záppio**. Popular with evening and weekend strollers, they're more open, and more formally laid out. The Záppio itself, an imposing Neoclassical edifice originally built as an exhibition hall, is not open to the public. Although it has no permanent function, the building has taken on prestigious roles such as the headquarters for both the Greek presidency of the European Union and of the 2004 Olympic bid, and is frequently put to use for conventions and exhibitions.

HADRIAN'S ARCH

Leofóros Amalías. MAP P.42–43, POCKET MAP D14

Hadrian's Arch stands in splendid isolation on what feels like one of the busiest corners in Athens, where Odhós Syngroú arrives in the centre of town. With the traffic roaring by, this is not somewhere you are tempted to linger – but it's definitely worth a look on your way to the Temple of Olympian Zeus.

The arch, eighteen metres high, was erected in honour of the emperor to mark the edge of the Classical city and the beginning of his own. On the west side its frieze – damaged and hard to make out – is inscribed "This is Athens, the ancient city of Theseus", and on the other "This is the City of Hadrian and not of Theseus". With so little that's ancient remaining around it, this doesn't make immediate sense, but you can look up, westwards, to the Acropolis and in the other direction see the columns of the great temple completed by Hadrian. Many more Roman remains are thought to lie under the Záppio area, and over towards the old Olympic Stadium.

THE ROMAN BATHS

Vasilíssis Amalías, alongside the Záppio gardens. MAP P.75, POCKET MAP E13

As the inscription on Hadrian's Arch suggests, Roman Athens expanded beyond the Classical Greek city to cover much of the area around the National Gardens. The most concrete evidence of this lies in a large **Roman baths complex** that was discovered during excavations for the Metro, 100m or so north of Hadrian's Arch. Dating originally from the late third century AD and substantially expanded over succeeding centuries, the excavated baths are visible, behind railings and some way below street level, alongside the busy avenue. Complete rooms have been well preserved and are now exposed to the gaze.

TEMPLE OF OLYMPIAN ZEUS

Entrance on Vasilíssis Ólgas. Daily: April–Sept 8am–7.30pm; Oct–March 8.30am–3pm. €2, or joint Acropolis ticket. MAP P.75, POCKET MAP E14

The colossal pillars of the **Temple of Olympian Zeus** – also known as the Olympieion – stand in the middle of a huge, dusty clearing with excellent views of the Acropolis and constant traffic noise. One of the largest temples in the ancient world – and according to Livy "the only temple on earth to do justice to the god" – it was dedicated by Hadrian in 131 AD, almost 700 years after the tyrant Peisistratos had begun work on it. Hadrian marked the occasion by contributing an enormous statue of Zeus and an equally monumental one of himself, although both have since been lost. The hubristic peril of building on such a scale was clear from the start: Peisistratos' original work was continued by his sons, but on their overthrow the work was abandoned, and the completed portion viewed for centuries as a symbol of tyranny. Hadrian's temple, in turn, survived little more than a century before being seriously damaged in barbarian attacks on Athens.

Today, just fifteen of the temple's original 104 marble pillars remain erect. To the north of the temple enclosure, by the site entrance, are various excavated remains including another impressive Roman bath complex. The south side of the enclosure overlooks a further area of excavation (not open to the public) where both Roman and much earlier buildings have been revealed.

THE ROMAN BATHS

Shops

ARISTON

Voúlis 10, cnr Karayeóryi Servías.
MAP P.75, POCKET MAP D12

Part of a small chain of local
zaharoplastía (cake shops),
with excellent value sweet and
savoury pies, biscuits, cakes and
old-fashioned fruit jelly sweets.

ATTICA

Panepistimíou 9. Mon–Fri 10am–9pm, Sat
10am–7pm. MAP P.75, POCKET MAP E11

Athens' prime fashion department store, with the finest
window displays in the city and
a huge branch of upmarket café
Zonar's on the ground floor.

KORI

Mitropóleos 13 and Voúlis. MAP P.75, POCKET
MAP D12

Very high-standard jewellery
and crafts in silver, gold and
ceramic, with prices to match.
Beautiful, original designs with
some traditional influences.

MASTIHASHOP

Panepistimíou, cnr Kriezótou ⓦ www
.mastihashop.com. MAP P.75, POCKET MAP E11

Mastiha is the resin of the
mastic tree from the island of
Chios, a traditional flavouring
and natural remedy. Here all
sorts of mastiha products – from
cosmetics to gourmet delicacies
– are sold in designer packaging.

Cafés and restaurants

CIBUS

Záppio gardens on the east side of the
Záppio ☎ 210 33 69 300, ⓦ www.aeglizappiou
.gr. Daily 12.30–4.30pm & 8pm–1am.
MAP P.75, POCKET MAP F14

Pricey, smart restaurant with a
fabulous setting, allegedly the

MASTIHASHOP

haunt of the rich and famous.
"Modern Mediterranean" food,
which here means Greek with
French and Italian influences.
It's part of the Aigli complex,
which also houses a café-bar
(*Lallabai*) and open-air cinema.

EVEREST

Ermoú 2, Platía Sindágmatos. 24hr daily.
MAP P.75, POCKET MAP E12

A branch of the ubiquitous
sandwich chain that's always
busy. While you can eat in (or
on the noisy pavement), you
may prefer to collect a picnic to
take to the National Gardens.

GLIKOYENESIS

Karayeóryi Servías 9, cnr Voúlis. MAP P.75,
POCKET MAP D12

Handy for Sýndagma and the
local shops, with excellent
coffee, sandwiches, salads and
cake by day, and cocktails at
night.

OASIS

West side of National Gardens, opposite cnr
of Amalías and Filellínon. Closed in winter.
MAP P.75, POCKET MAP E13

This café just off the main
avenue is an unexpected haven,
with light meals – sandwiches,
pizza, pasta – as well as ice
cream and drinks in the shade.

Platía Omonías and the bazaar

Platía Omonías (Omonía Square) and its surroundings represent the gritty, commercial side of Athens. Here the grand avenues imagined by the nineteenth-century planners have been subverted by time and the realities of daily life. Leaving Sýndagma on Stadhíou or Panepistimíou, there are at first grandiose mansions – some converted to museums – squares with open vistas, and chichi shopping: you don't have to go far, though, before the shops get smaller, the stoas more run down, the buildings less shiny.

Heading up from Monastiráki, the **bazaar area** around Odhós Athinás is home to a bustling series of markets and small stores spilling into the streets and offering some of urban Athens' most compelling sights and sounds, as well as an ethnic mix that is a rare reminder of Greece's traditional role as a meeting place of East and West. It's also a neighbourhood being increasingly recolonized by the drug addicts and prostitutes who were cleared out in time for the Olympics.

THE BAZAAR

MAP P.82, POCKET MAP C10

The modern market or **bazaar** is concentrated on Athinás and Eólou streets. Here the stores, though stocked mainly with imported manufactured goods, still reflect their origins in the Oriental souk system, where each street has a concentration of particular stores and wares. Hence the lower end of Athinás is dedicated to tools; food stores are gathered around the central market in the middle, especially along Evripídhou; there's glass to the west; paint and brasswork to the east; and clothes in Eólou and Ayíou Márkou.

At the heart of the area lies the **meat and seafood market**, set in a grand nineteenth-century building. Its fretted iron awnings shelter forests of carcasses and mounds of hearts, livers and ears – no place for the squeamish. In the middle section of the hall is the fish market, with all manner of bounty from the sea glistening on marble slabs.

SPICE SHOP, CENTRAL BAZAAR

Across Athinás from here, the **fruit and vegetable bazaar** is a riot of colours and noise, as the vendors shout their wares. In the surrounding streets grocers pile their stalls high with sacks of pulses, salt cod, barrels of olives and wheels of cheese.

ODHÓS EÓLOU AND THE FLOWER MARKET

MAP P.82, POCKET MAP C11

Odhós Eólou seems far less frantic than parallel Athinás, partly because it is pedestrianized. Local businesses take advantage of this, with café tables in the street, and benches to rest on. Its gentler nature perhaps reflects the goods sold here: where Athinás has power tools and raw meat, Eólou offers clothes and the **flower market**. The latter, gathered around the church of Ayía Iríni at the southern end of the street, has stalls through the week but is at its best and busiest on a Sunday morning.

The sight of the Acropolis from Eólou as you approached Athens in ancient times must have been awe-inspiring, and the street still has impressive **views** today, with the Erechtheion's slender columns and pediment peeking over the edge of the crag straight ahead.

PLATÍA KÓTZIA

MAP P.82, POCKET MAP C10

At the northern end of Odhós Eólou, **Platía Kótzia** is a formal enclave surrounded by the town hall and the weighty Neoclassical buildings of the National Bank. It's a rare glimpse of elegant old Athens, spoiled only by the crumbling modern blocks above the Post Office. In the middle of the square a large section of **ancient road** has been uncovered and fenced off – numerous

THE FISH MARKET

tombs and small buildings lie alongside it. This road, just outside the walls, once led to one of the main gates of ancient Athens and this too has recently been excavated, during building work for a new Stock Exchange. You can see it underneath the new building, between Platía Kótzia and Sofokléous; nearby, more sections of the ancient road and a drainage system are visible under glass pyramids in the middle of the street.

NATIONAL HISTORICAL MUSEUM

Stadhíou 13, Platía Kolokotróni.
Tues–Sun 9am–2pm. €3, free on Sun.
MAP P.82, POCKET MAP E11

Occupying a building that housed the Greek parliament from 1874 until 1935, the **National Historical Museum** focuses on Greek history from the fall of Constantinople to the reign of King Otto, with particular emphasis on the Byzantine era. There's also a strong section on the War of Independence that includes Byron's sword and helmet.

Platía Omonías and the bazaar

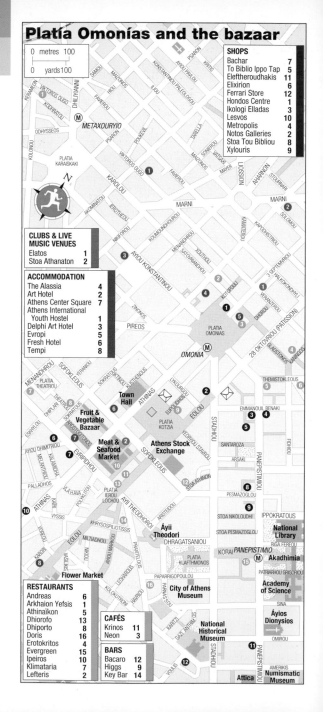

0 metres 100
0 yards 100

SHOPS
Bachar	7
To Biblio Ippo Tap	5
Eleftheroudhakis	11
Elixirion	6
Ferrari Store	12
Hondos Centre	1
Ikologi Elladas	3
Lesvos	10
Metropolis	4
Notos Galleries	2
Stoa Tou Bibliou	8
Xylouris	9

CLUBS & LIVE MUSIC VENUES
Elatos	1
Stoa Athanaton	2

ACCOMMODATION
The Alassia	4
Art Hotel	2
Athens Center Square	7
Athens International Youth Hostel	1
Delphi Art Hotel	3
Evropi	5
Fresh Hotel	6
Tempi	8

RESTAURANTS
Andreas	6
Arkhaion Yefsis	1
Athinaïkon	5
Dhiorofo	13
Dhiporto	8
Doris	16
Erotokritos	4
Evergreen	15
Ipeiros	10
Klimataria	7
Lefteris	2

CAFÉS
Krinos	11
Neon	3

BARS
Bacaro	12
Higgs	9
Key Bar	14

THE NATIONAL LIBRARY

PLATÍA KLAFTHOMÓNOS

MAP P.82, POCKET MAP D11

Platía Klafthomónos offers a wonderful view towards three grand Neoclassical buildings on Panepistimíou. Here the planners' conceptualization of the capital of newly independent Greece can for once be seen more or less as they envisaged it, blending the nation's Classical heritage with modern, Western values. As you look up you see, from the left, the sober grey marble of the **National Library**, the rather racier **Akadhimía** (University), enlivened by frescoes depicting King Otto surrounded by ancient Greek gods and heroes, and the frankly over-the-top **Academy of Science** with its pediment friezes and giant statues of Athena and Apollo. The garish decoration gives an alarming impression of what the Classical monuments might have looked like when their paintwork was intact.

CITY OF ATHENS MUSEUM

Paparigopoúlou 7, Platía Klafthomónos ⓦ www.athenscitymuseum.gr. Mon & Wed–Fri 9am–4pm, Sat & Sun 10am–3pm. €3. MAP P.82, POCKET MAP D11

The **City of Athens Museum** is housed in two of the city's oldest mansions, connected by a covered bridge. The main building was the residence of King Otto in the 1830s before his new palace was completed, and its exhibits cover Athens' history from Otto's time onwards. Some of the rooms have been restored to their state when the royals lived here, with exquisite period furnishings; the second building, too, is furnished with antiques to represent the lifestyle of the nineteenth-century aristocracy. On the walls are many artworks featuring the city, as well as a model of Athens in 1842, with just three hundred houses. A section of the ancient city walls can be seen in the basement.

NUMISMATIC MUSEUM

Panepistimíou 12. Tues–Sun 8.30am–3pm. €3. MAP P.82, POCKET MAP E11

This collection of over 600,000 **coins** and related artefacts – weights, lead stamps, medals, precious stones and a rich archive of documents – dates from Mycenaean times through to the modern era. The **building** itself, the magnificent former home of the German archeologist Heinrich Schliemann (excavator of Troy and Mycenae), is a substantial part of the attraction.

BACHAR

Shops

BACHAR

Evripídhou 31. MAP P.82, POCKET MAP C10
A shop from another age: grains, seeds, candles, aromatic bags of teas, herbs and medicinal remedies are doled out from vast sacks.

TO BIBLIO IPPO TAP

Panepistimíou 57, in the arcade. MAP P.82, POCKET MAP E4
High-quality outlet for official archeological-service publications – including guides to many obscure sites – that also sells first-rate museum reproductions.

ELEFTHEROUDHAKIS

Panepistimíou 17. Mon–Fri 9am–9pm; Sat 9am–6pm. MAP P.82, POCKET MAP E11
Seven floors of books, with plenty in English; there's a travel section on the top floor, and a good café on the sixth.

ELIXIRION

Evripídhou 41. MAP P.82, POCKET MAP C10
Old-fashioned store with magnificent original fittings. Herbs, dried fruit and garlic hang from the ceiling; you can buy teas, spices, grinders, dried fruits and honey as souvenirs.

FERRARI STORE

Kolokotróni 5, cnr Voúlis.
MAP P.82, POCKET MAP D11
Ferrari-branded gear from stuffed toys to watches, laptops to leather jackets, plus a Schumacher F1 car to drool over.

HONDOS CENTRE

Platía Omonías 4. MAP P.82, POCKET MAP D3
The city's top department store; though it's no Harrods – low-ceilinged, cramped and crowded. Reasonably priced, it stocks just about everything you could want and has several floors of clothes, as well as a café with Acropolis views.

IKOLOGI ELLADAS

Panepistimíou 57. MAP P.82, POCKET MAP E4
A big health-food supermarket with alternative medicine practitioners in-store, plus a café serving freshly-squeezed juices and vegetarian and organic foods to eat in or take away.

LESVOS

Athinás 33. MAP P.82, POCKET MAP C11
This glossy and somewhat touristy deli sells high-quality wine, honey, preserves and olive oil as well as bread, cheese and meats.

ELIXIRION

METROPOLIS

Panepistimíou 64. MAP P.82, POCKET MAP E4

Major city-centre branch of a Greek music chain, with four floors of mainstream music on CD, as well as DVDs and games. Concert tickets are also sold here.

NOTOS GALLERIES

Eólou 99. Mon & Wed 10am–7pm, Tues, Thurs & Fri 10am–9pm, Sat 10am–6pm.
MAP P.82, POCKET MAP D4

One of Athens' oldest and biggest department stores, stocking clothes, household goods, sports gear and electrical items at reasonable prices.

STOA TOU BIBLIOU

Stoa entered from Panepistimíou 49 or Pesmazogloú 5. MAP P.82, POCKET MAP D10

A quiet arcade (or stoa) devoted entirely to books, with seating areas and frequent exhibitions. Almost all in Greek, but still worth a look – a couple of antiquarian dealers have old maps.

XYLOURIS

Panepistimíou 39, in the arcade.
MAP P.82, POCKET MAP D10

Run by the widow of the late, great Cretan singer Nikos Xylouris, this is one of the best places for finding Greek pop, folk and Cretan music.

Cafés

KRINOS

Eólou 87, behind the central market.
MAP P.82, POCKET MAP C10

Operating since 1922, though thanks to recent refurbishment the only signs of that are the old photos adorning the walls. Still popular for old-fashioned treats like *loukoumádhes* (pastry puffs soaked in honey-citrus syrup and dusted in cinnamon) and *bougátsa*, as well as *tirópittes*, sandwiches and ice cream.

NEON

Dhórou 1, Platía Omonías 7.
MAP P.82, POCKET MAP D4

Modern interpretation of a traditional *kafenío* in a carefully restored Neoclassical building. The original *Neon* was something of an Athens institution, and there are still plenty of old men here drinking traditional Greek coffee. But the menu has been updated and this elegant escape also offers cappuccinos, sandwiches and simple food like moussaka and pasta at reasonable prices.

Restaurants

ANDREAS

Themistokléous 18 ☎ 210 38 21 522.
Lunch & dinner Mon–Sat, lunch Sun.
MAP P.82, POCKET MAP E4

A traditional ouzerí, specializing in fish dishes such as mussels and octopus fritters, that's popular for long weekday lunches, though also open in the evening.

ARKHAION YEFSIS

Kodhrátou 22, Metaxouryío ☎ 210 52 39 661.
ⓦ www.arxaion.gr. Lunch & dinner daily.
MAP P.82, POCKET MAP C3

The name means "ancient tastes" and this highly original restaurant claims to serve ancient Greek food, based on evidence from contemporary writings. It certainly makes for an enjoyable evening, in a lovely setting with bare stone walls, statues, flaming torches and a courtyard. Dishes include wild-boar cutlets and goat leg with mashed vegetables, cheese, garlic and honey (€27 for two), as well as plenty of less meaty options.

ATHINAÏKON

retsina is enjoyed by market workers as well as tourists and office suits, and, as the afternoon wears on, impromptu music often breaks out.

DORIS

Praxitélous 30 ☎ 210 32 32 671. Mon–Sat 8.30am–6.30pm. MAP P.82, POCKET MAP D11

A straightforward, reliable place that has been serving for decades. Famous for its *loukoumádhes* (pastry puffs soaked in syrup), but also serves grills and baked dishes.

EROTOKRITOS

Káningos 3 ☎ 210 38 12 583. Mon–Sat 8.30am–6.30pm. MAP P.82, POCKET MAP E3

The streets around Omónia are full of fast-food lunch places. This is one of the bigger ones, specializing in kebabs, sausages and *yíros*, with plenty of tables inside, as well as outside on a pedestrianized street.

EVERGREEN

Koraï 4, in Galeria Koraï off Platía Koraï. 24hr daily. MAP P.82, POCKET MAP D10

Healthy, fast food-style sandwiches, salads, juices, smoothies and coffee. Tables

ATHINAÏKON

Themistokléous 2, cnr Panepistimíou ☎ 210 38 38 485. Lunch & dinner Mon–Sat; closed Aug. MAP P.82, POCKET MAP E4

Long-established, old-fashioned *mezedhopolío* with a huge variety of good-sized, mid-priced *mezédhes*: seafood – such as shrimp croquettes and mussels simmered with cheese and peppers – is a speciality.

DHIOROFO

Eólou 77, cnr Evripídhou. Lunch & dinner daily. MAP P.82, POCKET MAP C10

A modern café-restaurant whose traditional-style daily lunchtime specials (€6–10) are popular with shoppers and local office workers. Tables on the street, as well as a quiet, air-conditioned interior.

DHIPORTO

Theátrou, cnr Sokrátous. Mon–Sat 6am–6pm. MAP P.82, POCKET MAP C10

Two brown-painted metal trapdoors in the pavement open to a steep stairway down into a basement that feels like it survives from an Athens of fifty years ago. Simple, inexpensive Greek food – soup, salad, fish – washed down with

DHIPORTO

out on the square, and the Galeria is full of other cafés.

IPEIROS

Southeast corner of the meat market. Open all day, every day, till late. MAP P.82, POCKET MAP C10

A favourite for late-night resuscitation or for a hangover cure the following morning, *Ipeiros* is an entirely traditional taverna. There's a wide range of excellent, inexpensive baked dishes that you can choose from the kitchen, but the soups are what this place is known for, above all *patsa*, a tripe soup that's renowned as a cure-all.

KLIMATARIA

Platía Theátrou 2 ☎ 210 32 16 629. Lunch Mon–Thurs & Sun, lunch & dinner Fri & Sat. MAP P.82, POCKET MAP B10

Friendly, old-fashioned taverna serving ample portions of traditional fare at reasonable prices. The daily specials include excellent vegetable dishes, plus daily roast meats. Wine barrels are just about the only decoration, but there's courtyard seating in summer and live music at the end of the week.

LEFTERIS

Satovriándhou 20 ☎ 210 52 25 676. Lunch & dinner daily. MAP P.82, POCKET MAP D3

Very popular hole-in-the-wall *souvláki* place – eat standing up at high tables, or take away.

Bars

BACARO

Sofokléous 1 ☎ 210 32 11 882, ⓦ www .myspace.com/bacarolive. MAP P.82, POCKET MAP D10

Arty café-bar that's open all day and boasts live jazz – or occasionally blues or Latin music – virtually every night, usually with free entry.

HIGGS

Eupolídhos 4, Platía Kótzia ☎ 210 32 47 679 ⓦ www.higgs.gr. MAP P.82, POCKET MAP C10

Reinvention of a traditional *kafenío* as a fashionable café-bar with resident DJs from Wednesday to Sunday and frequent events. Tends to draw a professional crowd with a variety of dance-based music, and occasional forays into rock or African sounds.

KEY BAR

Praxitélous 37 ☎ 210 32 30 381. MAP P.82, POCKET MAP C11

The narrow frontage on a quiet street doesn't promise much, but with DJs nightly from 9pm, plus weekend afternoon parties, there's almost always something going on here. Busy with an after-work crowd early on, the music later can be anything from hip-hop to reggae, Sixties soul to post-punk.

Clubs and live music venues

ELATOS

Trítis Septemvríou 16 ☎ 210 52 34 262. Closed Wed. MAP P.82, POCKET MAP D3

There's an eclectic assortment of traditional music in this downtown basement club, going strong since 1918.

STOA ATHANATON

Sofokléous 19, at entrance to the meat market ☎ 210 32 14 362. 3–6pm & midnight–6am; closed Sun & May–Aug. MAP P.82, POCKET MAP C11

This rebétika place fronted by *bouzoúki* veterans Hondronakos and company is one of the city's best known. There's good taverna food at reasonable prices, but drinks are expensive.

The Archeological Museum, Exárhia and Neápoli

In northern Athens there's just one sight of any note, and it is an essential stop on any visit to Athens, however brief. The fabulous National Archeological Museum is simply the finest collection of ancient Greek artefacts anywhere, and regarded as among the top ten museums in the world. However high your expectations, the museum seems effortlessly to surpass them, full of objects that seem familiar, so often have you seen them in pictures or reproductions.

There are few specific sights otherwise, but it's a rewarding part of the city for a wander – restaurants, bars, cafés and bookshops abound. **Exárhia**, fifty-odd blocks squeezed between the National Archeological Museum and Lófos tou Stréfi, is one of the city's liveliest neighbourhoods, especially at night. Traditionally the home of anarchists, revolutionaries, artists, students and anyone seeking an anti-establishment lifestyle in a conformist city, Exárhia is pretty tame these days, but it's still the closest thing in central Athens to an "alternative" neighbourhood. Nearby **Neápoli** is home to a swathe of good, low-key tavernas, many featuring rebétika-style atmosphere and sometimes the music itself.

Just above this, the little-visited **Stréfis Hill** (Lófos tou Stréfi) provides some great views and a welcome break from the densely packed streets and dull apartment blocks surrounding it.

JEWELLERY AT THE NATIONAL ARCHEOLOGICAL MUSEUM

NATIONAL ARCHEOLOGICAL MUSEUM

Patission 44 ⓦ www.culture.gr. Mon 1.30–7.30pm, Tues–Sun 8.30am–7.30pm; closes 3pm Tues–Sun in winter. €7.
MAP P.90–91, POCKET MAP E2

The **National Archeological Museum** is an unrivalled treasure-house of ancient Greek art. The biggest crowd-pullers are the **Mycenaean Halls**, directly ahead of you as you enter, including the gold funerary "Mask of Agamemnon" and large quantities of other intricate objects from the fifteenth and fourteenth centuries BC. Other highlights include a golden-horned Bull's Head; gold jewellery including a diadem and a gold-foil cover for the body of an infant from Grave III (the "Grave of the Women"); the Acropolis Treasure of gold goblets, signet rings and jewellery; and dozens of examples of the Mycenaeans' consummate art-intricate, small-scale decoration of rings, cups, seals and inlaid daggers. There's work in silver, ivory, bronze and boars' tusks as well, plus baked tablets of Linear B, the earliest Greek writing (mainly accounting records) and Cretan-style frescoes depicting chariot-borne women watching spotted hounds in pursuit of boar and bull-vaulting.

Still-earlier Greece is represented in the adjoining rooms. Room 5 covers **Neolithic pottery** and stone tools from Attica and elsewhere, and runs through to the early Bronze Age. Room 6 is home to a large collection of **Cycladic art** from the Aegean islands.

The largest part of the collection, though, is **sculpture**, following a broadly chronological arrangement around the main halls.

Highlights include a statue of a *kore* (maiden) from Merenda (Myrrhinous) in Attica, in room 11. Nearby is a wonderful grave stele of a young *doryphoros* (spear-bearer) against a red background. Room 13 has the stele of a young warrior, with delicately carved beard, hair and tunic-folds.

Of the massive Classical collection the **bronzes** stand out: in particular the *Statue of Poseidon*, poised to throw his trident, athlete's body perfectly balanced, and the *Little Jockey of Artemission*, both of them recovered from a wreck off Évvia in the 1920s. Room 28 has some fine, fourth-century-BC bronzes including the *Antikithira Youth*, thought to depict either Perseus or Paris, from yet another shipwreck, off Antikithira, and the bronze *Head of a Boxer*, burly and battered. Still more naturalistic is the third-century-BC bronze head of a *Philosopher*, nearby, with furrowed brow and unkempt hair.

Less visited, but still extremely worthwhile, are the collections at the rear of the museum. These include the Stathatos collection, with more exquisite **jewellery**; a wonderful **Egyptian** collection, including beautiful, fragile wooden sculptures; and displays of **Greek bronze-work**, featuring a reconstructed chariot and the extraordinary **Antikithira Mechanism**, a sophisticated astronomical computer 1500 years ahead of its time. Upstairs are a vast collection of **vases**, both fabulous and fascinating, and a room devoted to the **excavations at Thirá** (Santorini), where some of the famous frescoes discovered there are displayed.

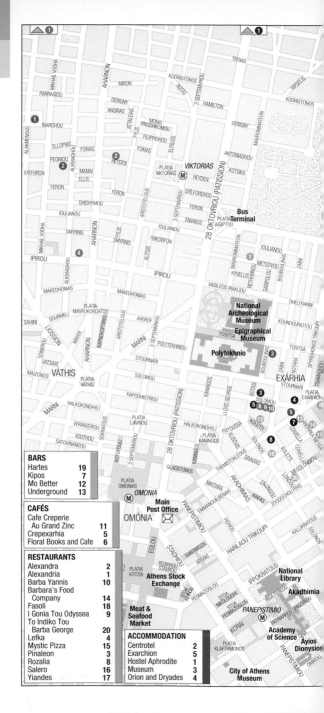

BARS

Hartes	19
Kipos	7
Mo Better	12
Underground	13

CAFÉS

Cafe Creperie Au Grand Zinc	11
Crepexarhia	5
Floral Books and Cafe	6

RESTAURANTS

Alexandra	2
Alexandria	1
Barba Yannis	10
Barbara's Food Company	14
Fasoli	18
I Gonia Tou Odyssea	9
To Indiko Tou Barba George	20
Lefka	4
Mystic Pizza	15
Pinaleon	3
Rozalia	8
Salero	16
Yiandes	17

ACCOMMODATION

Centrotel	2
Exarchion	5
Hostel Aphrodite	1
Museum	3
Orion and Dryades	4

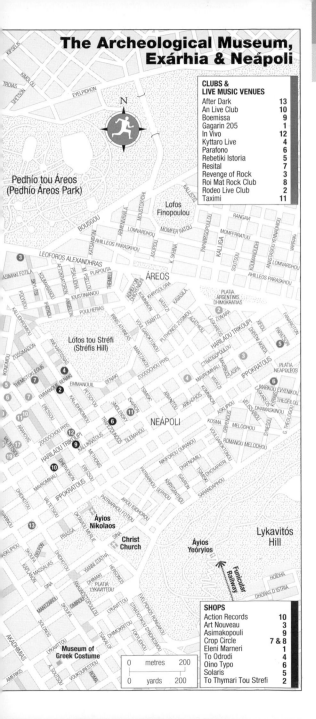

The Archeological Museum, Exárhia & Neápoli

CLUBS & LIVE MUSIC VENUES

After Dark	13
An Live Club	10
Boemissa	9
Gagarin 205	1
In Vivo	12
Kyttaro Live	4
Parafono	6
Rebetiki Istoria	5
Resital	7
Revenge of Rock	3
Roi Mat Rock Club	8
Rodeo Live Club	2
Taximi	11

Pedhío tou Áreos
(Pedhío Áreos Park)

Lofos Finopoulou

ÁREOS

Lófos tou Stréfi
(Stréfis Hill)

NEÁPOLI

PLATIA
ARGENTINIS
DHIMOKRATIAS

PLATIA
NEÁPOLEOS

Áyios
Nikolaos

Christ
Church

Áyios
Yeóryios

Lykavitós
Hill

Funicular
Railway

Museum of
Greek Costume

PLATIA
LYKAVITTOU

SHOPS

Action Records	10
Art Nouveau	3
Asimakopouli	9
Crop Circle	7 & 8
Eleni Marneri	1
To Odrodi	4
Oino Typo	6
Solaris	5
To Thymari Tou Strefi	2

0	metres	200
0	yards	200

POLYTEKHNÍO

Patission 42. MAP P.90–91, POCKET MAP E3

The Neoclassical building housing the **Polytechnic** (Polytekhnío), the university's school of engineering and science, is not open to visits, but it played a significant role in recent Greek history. In November 1973 students here launched a protest against the repressive regime of the colonels, occupying the building and broadcasting calls for mass resistance. On the night of November 17, snipers were positioned in neighbouring houses and ordered to fire into the court-yards while a tank broke down the entrance gate and the buildings were stormed. Even today nobody knows how many of the unarmed students were killed – estimates range from twenty to three hundred. The protest arguably marked the beginning of the end for the colonels; its anniversary is still commemorated by marches and sombre remembrance ceremonies.

VIEW OF THE ACROPOLIS FROM STRÉFIS HILL

EPIGRAPHICAL MUSEUM

Tosítsa 1. Tues–Sun 8.30am–3pm. Free. MAP P.90–91, POCKET MAP E3

The **Epigraphical Museum** occupies part of the National Archeological Museum building, with a separate entrance at the side. Over 13,000 inscriptions trace the development of the Greek language and alphabet; most are carved into marble or stone, but there's also stamped pottery and tiles, and various examples of early writing. All fairly specialist, but it's interesting to see the development in the use of language, from simple lists and accounts to laws, treaties, letters and funeral tributes.

STRÉFIS HILL

MAP P.90–91, POCKET MAP F3

Overlooking Neápoli, the little-visited **Stréfis Hill** (Lófos tou Stréfi) rises above the residential streets that surround it. A labyrinth of paths leads up to the low summit, from where there are unexpectedly wonderful **views** – above all of the Acropolis with the Saronic Gulf and islands behind, but also across to nearby Lykavitós. Watch out for unguarded drops near the top and stick to the main paths as you walk up to avoid one of the more obvious signs of the area's alternative lifestyle, discarded hypodermics.

PEDHÍO TOU ÁREOS

MAP P.90–91, POCKET MAP F2

One of the few green areas in the centre of Athens, the **Pedhío tou Áreos** (Plain of Mars) is a substantial park of trees, gardens and meandering paths. A long boulevard bisects the park, with a line of statues of heroes of the Greek War of Independence keeping silent vigil over the strolling visitors.

Shops

ACTION RECORDS

Mavromiháli 51. MAP P.90–91, POCKET MAP F4
Specialist music shop dealing in garage, beat, psychedelic, folk and progressive music (mainly on vinyl) from around the world. They also have their own recording label.

ART NOUVEAU

Solomoú 23, Exárhia. MAP P.90–91, POCKET MAP E3
Amazing collection of classic vinyl, new and secondhand. Mostly traditional rock, but also 1960s soul and all sorts of other gems.

ASIMAKOPOULI

Hariláou Trikoúpi 82. MAP P.90–91, POCKET MAP F3
One of the best patisseries in the city, offering a rich variety of fresh, high-quality sweets, cakes, home-made ice cream and excellent *tsoureki* (sweet bread).

CROP CIRCLE

Themistokléous 52 and 66. MAP P.90–91, POCKET MAP E3
Reasonably priced vintage clothing and ethnic jewellery. The branch higher up the hill sells new stock, the lower one vintage.

CROP CIRCLE

Street markets

One of the finest local street markets in Athens, mainly for fresh fruit and veg, takes over **Odhós Kallidhromíou**, in Neápoli beneath the Lófos Stréfi, every Saturday.

ELENI MARNERI

Agathoupóleos 3, Kypséli (off 28 Oktovríou, north of Metro Viktorías). MAP P.90–91, POCKET MAP E1
A beautiful contemporary jewellery shop whose decor reflects the innovative style of the designers. A great selection and occasional exhibitions.

TO ODRODI

Solomoú 4. MAP P.90–91, POCKET MAP E3
Kit yourself out like an Exarhía anarcho-hippy at this shop, selling everything from bongs, nose studs and cheap jewellery to gifts and clothing.

OINO TYPO

Hariláou Trikoúpi 98. MAP P.90–91, POCKET MAP G3
Excellent wine merchant with over fifty varieties of Greece's famous barreled wines (you can fill your own bottle), as well as 1200 international bottled wines.

SOLARIS

Botási 6. MAP P.90–91, POCKET MAP E3
Comics old and new, as well as graphic novels, models of characters and other paraphernalia.

TO THYMARI TOU STREFI

Kallidhromíou 51A. MAP P.90–91, POCKET MAP F3
A lovely retro *pantopolío* (corner store, literally a store that sells everything) selling traditional Greek preserves, honey, nuts, dried fruit, cheese, olives and olive oil among much else.

Cafés

CAFÉ CREPERIE AU GRAND ZINC

Emmanouíl Benáki 88. MAP P.90–91, POCKET MAP F3

This café's cosy, quiet and wood-lined interior makes a peaceful stop for coffee and crêpes, often to the background of a little jazz.

CREPEXARHIA

Platía Exarhíon, cnr Themistokléous and Ikonómou. MAP P.90–91, POCKET MAP F3

Simple crêperie in a busy corner of the square, also serving coffee, sandwiches and ice cream.

FLORAL BOOKS AND CAFE

Themistokléous 80, Platía Exarhíon
Ⓦ www.floralcafe.gr. MAP P.90–91, POCKET MAP F3

Spacious and comfortable bookstore/café, devoting roughly equal space to each activity. Coffee, juices and snacks in the day, with more of a cocktail bar atmosphere at night, and occasional live music too.

Restaurants

ALEXANDRA

Zonará 21, off Leofóros Alexandhrás
☎ 210 64 20 874, Ⓦ www.alexandra
-restaurant.gr. Lunch & dinner Mon–Sat.
MAP P.90–91, POCKET MAP G2

Always busy with locals despite a rather obscure location, this modernized mansion has smart decor, a veranda in summer, and occasional music. The food is imaginative and not too pricey: as well as excellent salads, grills and fish, there are more exotic offerings like aubergine stuffed with veal and sun-dried tomato, seafood spaghetti cooked in paper, and barbecued pork with lemon and mushrooms.

BARBA YIANNIS

ALEXANDRIA

Metsóvou 13, cnr Rethýmnou
☎ 210 82 10 004. Lunch & dinner Mon–Sat;
closed Aug. MAP P.90–91, POCKET MAP E2

Greek/Middle Eastern food with an Egyptian theme and old colonial feel to the decor – palms and ceiling fans and a pleasant courtyard garden. Booking advised.

BARBA YIANNIS

Emmanouíl Benáki 94 ☎ 210 33 00 185.
Open all day, every day, until late.
MAP P.90–91, POCKET MAP F3

Popular neighbourhood treasure with a varied daily menu of home-style oven-cooked food (displayed in large pots near entrance) in a relaxed atmosphere, aided and abetted by barrelled wine. Tables on pedestrianized street in summer.

BARBARA'S FOOD COMPANY

Emmanouíl Benáki 63–65 ☎ 210 38 05 004.
Lunch & dinner daily. MAP P.90–91, POCKET MAP F3

Colourful café-restaurant with wonderful salads and pasta dishes, plus daily specials from around the world, from meatballs to won-tons.

FASOLI

Emmanouíl Benáki 45, Exárhia
☎ 210 33 00 010. Lunch & dinner daily.
MAP P.90–91, POCKET MAP E3

Fashionable, youthful *estiatório* with all-white decor and

twinkly lights strung about the place, serving tasty modern Greek food.

I GONIA TOU ODYSSEA

Arahóvis 59. Lunch & dinner daily.
MAP P.90–91, POCKET MAP F3

Mushroom *saganáki*, meatballs, spicy sausages and octopus are among the delights at this simple, old-fashioned ouzerí.

TO INDIKO TOU BARBA GEORGE

Messolongíou 4. Lunch & dinner daily.
MAP P.90–91, POCKET MAP E4

Basic two-table Indian restaurant livening up the tastebuds of Exárhia with its chicken curries and vegetable biryani. Also takeaways, mainly in the form of nan wraps.

LEFKA

Mavromiháli 121 ☎ 210 36 14 038.
Lunch & dinner Mon–Sat, lunch Sun.
MAP P.90–91, POCKET MAP G3

Beloved old taverna with great *fáva* (hummus-like bean purée), black-eyed beans and baked and grilled meat with barrelled retsina. Summer seating in a huge garden enclosed by barrels.

MYSTIC PIZZA

Emmanouíl Benáki 76, Exárhia
☎ 210 38 39 500. Lunch & dinner daily.
MAP P.90–91, POCKET MAP F3

Tiny, unpretentious place serving pasta and salads as well as excellent pizzas (mostly €8–9). The flour is made from hemp (cannabis) seeds, which they claim has both health and environmental benefits. Takeaway and delivery too.

PINALEON

Mavromiháli 152 ☎ 210 64 40 945.
Lunch & dinner daily; closed June–Sept.
MAP P.90–91, POCKET MAP G3

A classic old-style taverna, serving rich *mezédhes* and meaty entrées, washed down with wine, lovingly brewed by the chef/owner from Híos. Book in advance.

ROZALIA

Valtetsíou 58 ☎ 210 33 02 933. Lunch & dinner daily. MAP P.90–91, POCKET MAP F3

Popular mid-range taverna, with excellent chicken and barrelled wine. You order *mezédhes* from the tray as the waiters thread their way through the throng; also grilled fish and meat. In summer you can dine in the garden.

SALERO

Valtetsíou 51 ☎ 210 38 13 358. Lunch & dinner daily. MAP P.90–91, POCKET MAP F3

Lively, modern Spanish wine and tapas bar on two storeys, plus a courtyard. The tapas have a distinctly Greek flavour, and there's a cocktail happy hour from 7 to 10pm.

YIANDES

Valtetsíou 44 ☎ 210 33 01 369. Lunch & dinner daily. MAP P.90–91, POCKET MAP F3

Modern and, for Exárhia, upmarket place serving excellent, modern Greek food with Asian influences. Pleasant courtyard too.

ROZALIA

Bars

HARTES

Valtetsíou 35, cnr Zoodóchou Piyís
☎ 210 33 04 778. MAP P.90–91, POCKET MAP F3

A crowded, early-evening meeting place, this café-bar has a great location for people-watching from its outdoor tables. Good rock sounds too.

KIPOS

Emmanouíl Benáki 87 ☎ 210 38 13 685. From 6pm, closed Sun. MAP P.90–91, POCKET MAP F3

Café-bar housed in an old mansion with numerous rooms featuring different musical genres, plus a pleasant court-yard. Upstairs is *Decadence*, a long-established rock-based club that's relocated here.

MO BETTER

Kolétti 32 ☎ 210 38 12 981. Closed Sun. €6 entry includes drink. MAP P.90–91, POCKET MAP E3

Cramped but fun bar on the first floor of a Neoclassical building, where the action starts late. Alternative, 80s and 90s rock, plus hip-hop, garage, punk and indie.

UNDERGROUND

A Metaxá 25, cnr Platía Exarhíon.
MAP P.90–91, POCKET MAP F3

By day a café-bar with a rock soundtrack, *Underground* transforms into a heavy metal and thrash club from around 11pm – loud and sweaty.

Clubs and live music venues

AFTER DARK

Dhiodótou 31 ☎ 210 36 06 460, Ⓦwww .afterdark.gr. From 10pm. €5–€8 entry.
MAP P.90–91, POCKET MAP F4

Indie bands, rock, blues and soul, and a young crowd.

AN LIVE CLUB

Solomoú 13–15 ☎ 210 33 05 056, Ⓦwww .anclub.gr. From 8pm. Typically €10 entry.
MAP P.90–91, POCKET MAP E3

Basement club featuring local and lesser-known foreign rock bands.

BOEMISSA

Solomoú 13–15 ☎ 210 38 38 803, Ⓦwww.boemissarebetika.gr. Tues–Sun 11pm–4am. Reservations recommended.
MAP P.90–91, POCKET MAP E3

Rebétika and laïká place popular with university students, who jam the dance floor and aisles, and inevitably end up dancing on the tables as well. Good company of musicians play music from all regions of Greece. Drinks €7: two-drink minimum. *Mezédhes* are served too.

GAGARIN 205

Liossíon 205, near Metro Attikís
☎ 210 85 47 601, Ⓦwww.gagarin205.gr.
MAP P.90–91, POCKET MAP C1

A long way north, but probably the finest venue for live rock in Athens, where some 2000 fans can crowd in to see the best touring indie bands as well as local talent and club nights.

IN VIVO

Harilάou Trikoúpi 79 ☎ 210 38 22 103, Ⓦwww.myspace.com/invivoliveclub. Open Oct–Jun, Fri & Sat from 11pm. Entry €6–15.
MAP P.90–91, POCKET MAP F3

Classy blues, jazz and rock acts are the order of the day at this intimate, friendly venue.

KYTTARO LIVE

Ipírou 48 ☎ 210 82 24 134, Ⓦwww.kyttaro live.gr. From 9pm. Entry charge varies €10–25.
MAP P.90–91, POCKET MAP D2

Mid-size, modern, galleried venue with live rock, punk and blues, plus Greek indie bands. Also DJ-led dance events.

PARAFONO

Asklipíou 130A ☎ 210 64 46 512, ⓦ www .parafono.gr. Daily from 9.30pm. Entry charge varies (around €10). MAP P.90–91, POCKET MAP H3

Excellent jazz and blues – mainly featuring local groups – in a congenial, small, cabaret-style club.

REBETIKI ISTORIA

Ippokrátous 181 ☎ 210 64 24 937. Closed Sun & July–Aug. MAP P.90–91, POCKET MAP H3

A lovely old house with traditional rebétika sounds from a good company led by Pavlos Vasileiou; drinks from €6, and tasty food is also served.

RESITAL

Eressoú 64 ☎ 210 38 05 556. MAP P.90–91, POCKET MAP F3

One of the longest-established music bars in Exárhia. The club is upstairs in an ivy-draped mansion, with over-the-top decor, 80s rock and jazz sounds, plus a roof terrace to escape it all.

REVENGE OF ROCK

Leofóros Alexandhrás 34, opposite Pedhío Áreos Park ☎ 210 88 30 695. MAP P.90–91, POCKET MAP F2

Large club with classic and hard rock sounds, and occasional live performances too.

RODEO LIVE CLUB

Héyden 34, Viktorías ☎ 210 88 14 702, ⓦ www.myspace.com/rodeoliveclub. From 9pm. Entry charge varies €12–25. MAP P.90–91, POCKET MAP D1

A top venue since the 1960s, and still going strong, with indie and rock bands entertaining a friendly, alternative crowd.

ROI MAT ROCK CLUB

Solomoú 17–19 ☎ 210 33 05 056, ⓦ www .roimatrockclub.gr. Wed–Sun late. Usually free entry. MAP P.90–91, POCKET MAP E3

Sweaty basement rock club that frequently hosts the after-parties from neighbouring *An Live Club* (see opposite), which shares the same management.

TAXIMI

Isávron 29B ☎ 210 36 39 919. Closed Sun & July–Aug. MAP P.90–91, POCKET MAP G3

This large, crowded rebétika salon on the third floor of a Neoclassical building seems to have been around for ever. It attracts a crowd of all ages; there's no cover charge, but drinks cost from €7 and pricey *mezédhes* are available too.

REBETIKI ISTORIA

Kolonáki and Lykavitós Hill

If you have money to spend, Kolonáki is the place to do it, catering as it does to every Western taste from fast food to high fashion. It's also from here that a funicular hauls you up Lykavitós Hill, where some of the best views of the city can be enjoyed. Close at hand, too, is a clutch of major museums.

At night the area comes to life, with plenty of upmarket bars, cafés and restaurants. Further east, the more modern neighbourhoods of **Ilísia** and **Ambelókipi** boast more busy bars and music clubs, as well as the **Mégaro Mousikís**, Athens' principal concert hall.

KOLONÁKI

MAP P.100–101, POCKET MAP G5–H5

Kolonáki is the city's most chic central address and shopping area. Walk up from Sýndagma, past the jewellery stores and luxury brands on Voukourestíou, and you can almost smell the money. The neighbourhood's lower limits are defined by **Akadhimías** and **Vasilíssis Sofías** streets, where grand Neoclassical palaces house embassies and museums. The middle stretches of the quarter are taken up with shops, while the highest, wonderfully located on the southwest-facing slopes of Lykavitós, looking out over the Acropolis and National Gardens, are purely residential.

The heart of it all is a square officially called Platía Filikís Eterías, but known to all as **Platía Kolonakíou**, after the ancient "little column" that hides in the trees on the southwest side. Dotted around the square are kiosks with stocks of foreign papers and magazines, or in the library of the British Council you can check out the British press for free. The surrounding cafés are almost invariably packed with Gucci-clad shoppers – you'll find better value if you move away from the square a little. In the dozens of small, upmarket shops the accent is firmly on fashion and designer gear, and a half-hour stroll around the neighbourhood will garner the whole gamut of consumer style.

For more random strolling, the highest tiers of Kolonáki can be very enjoyable, with steep streets ending in long flights of steps, planted with oleander and jasmine.

KOLONÁKI CAFÉ LIFE

LYKAVITÓS HILL

MAP P.100–101, POCKET MAP G4–J4

Lykavitós Hill offers tremendous views, particularly from late afternoon onwards – on a clear day you can see the mountains of the Peloponnese. After dark, the shimmering lights of Athens spread right across the Attica basin. To get to the summit you can take the **funicular** (daily 9am–2am; every 30min, more frequent at busy times; €6 return) or you can walk. The funicular begins its ascent from Odhós Aristípou, near the top of Ploutárhou. To get here is in itself something of a climb – though it doesn't look far from Kolonáki square, it's a steep ascent through the stepped residential streets. To do the whole journey the lazy way take bus #060 to the base of the funicular – this starts its journey at the terminus beside the National Archeological Museum and has handy stops on Akadhimías.

The principal path up the hill begins from the western end of Aristípou above Platía Dhexamenís, rambling through woods to the top. It's not as long or as hard a walk as it looks – easily done in twenty minutes – though the top half offers little shade.

On the summit, the brilliantly white chapel of **Áyios Yeóryios** dominates – a spectacular place to celebrate the saint's name-day (April 24). Just below it, *Orizontes* (p.108) is a pricey restaurant with an equally expensive café, both of which enjoy spectacular views. Over to the east a second, slightly lower peak is dominated by the open-air **Lykavitós Theatre**, used mainly for concerts from May to October. There's a road up to the theatre; head down in this direction to emerge in Kolonáki near the lovely little enclave that the British and American archeological schools have created for themselves on Odhós Souidhías.

Kolonáki and Lykavitós Hill

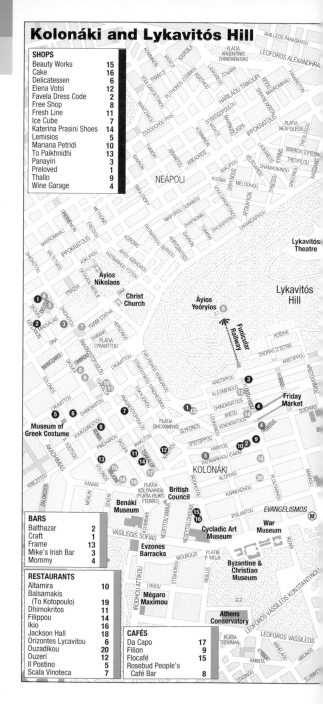

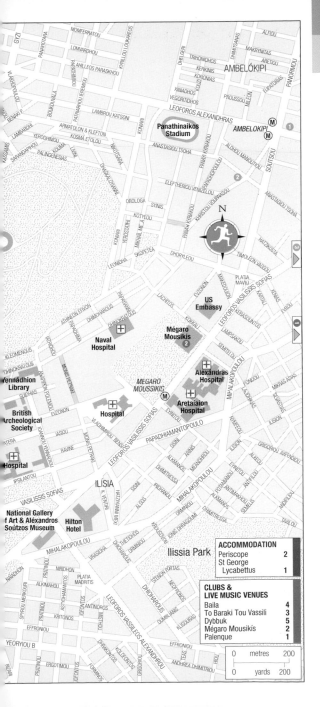

CLUBS & LIVE MUSIC VENUES	
Baila	4
To Baraki Tou Vassili	3
Dybbuk	5
Mégaro Mousikís	2
Palenque	1

ACCOMMODATION	
Periscope	2
St George Lycabettus	1

BENÁKI MUSEUM

BENÁKI MUSEUM

Koumbári 1, cnr Vasilíssis Sofías Ⓦ www
.benaki.gr. Mon, Wed, Fri & Sat 9am–5pm, Thurs
9am–midnight, Sun 9am–3pm. €6, temporary
exhibitions €3. MAP P.100–101, POCKET MAP G6

The often overlooked but fascinating **Benáki Museum** should
not be missed. Housing a private
collection donated to the state in
the 1950s by Antonis Benákis,
a wealthy cotton merchant, its
exhibits range from Mycenaean
jewellery, Greek costumes and
folk artefacts to memorabilia
from Byron and the Greek
War of Independence, as well
as jewellery from the Hélène
Stathatos collection.

Ancient finds are on the
lower floors and modern Greek
artefacts on the upper floors.
Among the more unusual items
are collections of early Greek
Gospels, liturgical vestments
and church ornaments rescued
by Greek refugees from Asia
Minor in 1922. There are also
dazzling embroideries and body
ornaments, and some unique
material on Cretan independence and its architect, the
statesman Elefthérios Venizélos.

An additional attraction,
especially if you've been
dodging traffic all day, is the
pricey rooftop **café**, with views
from the veranda over the
nearby National Gardens. The
museum **shop** stocks books on
Greek folk art, CDs of regional
music, and some great posters
and postcards.

CYCLADIC ART MUSEUM

Neofýtou Dhouká 4 Ⓦ www.cycladic-m.gr.
Mon, Wed, Fri & Sat 10am–5pm, Thurs
10am–8pm, Sun 11am–5pm. €7, Mon €3.50.
MAP P.100–101, POCKET MAP G6

The small, private **Goulandhrís
Museum of Cycladic and
Ancient Greek Art** is a beautifully presented collection
that includes objects from
the Cycladic civilization
(third millennium BC, from
the islands of the Cyclades
group), pre-Minoan Bronze
Age (second millennium BC)
and the period from the fall of
Mycenae to around 700 BC,
plus Archaic, Classical and
Hellenistic pottery.

The **Cycladic objects** are
on the first floor – above all
distinctive marble bowls and
folded-arm figurines (mostly
female) with sloping wedge
heads whose style influenced
twentieth-century artists like
Moore, Picasso and Brancusi.
The exact purpose of the
effigies is unknown but, given
their frequent discovery in
grave-barrows, it's possible that
they were spirit-world guides
for the deceased, substitutes
for the sacrifice of servants and
attendants, or representations
of the Earth Goddess. Their
clean, white simplicity is in
fact misleading, for they would
originally have been painted.
Look closely, and you can see
that many still bear traces.

Of the **ancient Greek art** on
the upper floors, the highlight
is the superb black-figure
pottery, especially a collection
of painted Classical-era bowls,

often showing two unrelated scenes on opposite sides; one of the star exhibits depicts revellers on one face and three men in cloaks conversing on the other. Others include, on the second floor, a depiction of Hephaistos' return to Olympus, with Hephaistos and Dionysos riding donkeys, and, on the top floor, a lovely *pyxis* with a lid of four horses.

On the ground floor and basement is a children's area and a **shop**, as well as a **café** (with good vegetarian choices) in an internal courtyard. From here a walkway connects to the nineteenth-century **Stathatos House**, magnificently restored to house exhibitions.

BYZANTINE AND CHRISTIAN MUSEUM

Vasilíssis Sofías 22 ⓦ www.byzantinemuseum .gr. Summer Tues–Sun 8.30am–7.30pm, winter Tues–Sun 8.30am–3pm. €4. MAP P.100–101, POCKET MAP H6

The **Byzantine and Christian Museum** is excellently displayed in a beautiful building, and its collection is far more wide-ranging than you might expect from the name. The setting is a peaceful, courtyarded villa that once belonged to the Duchesse de Plaisance, an extravagantly eccentric French-American philhellene and widow of a Napoleonic general who helped fund the War of Independence.

The exhibits start with art from the very earliest days of Christianity, whose fish and dove motifs can't disguise their extremely close parallels with Classical Greek objects. There are displays on everyday Byzantine life; reconstructions of parts of early churches (mosaic floors and chunks of masonry, some even from the Christian Parthenon); a Coptic section with antique clothing such as leather shoes decorated with gold leaf; and tombs in some of which offerings were left, again a reminder of a pagan heritage.

But the highlights are the **icons**, with the earliest being from the thirteenth and fourteenth centuries. There are dozens of lovely examples, many of them double-sided, some mounted to be carried in procession, and you can follow the development of their style from the simplicity of the earliest icons to the Renaissance-influenced selections from the sixteenth century. Alongside the icons are some fine **frescoes**, including an entire dome reconstructed inside the museum.

WAR MUSEUM

Cnr Vasilíssis Sofías & Rizári 2 ⓦ www.war museum.gr. Tues–Sat 9am–2pm, Sun 9.30am–2pm. €2. MAP P.100–101, POCKET MAP H6

The only "cultural" endowment of the 1967–74 junta, the **War Museum** becomes predictably militaristic and right-wing as it approaches modern events: the Asia Minor campaign, Greek forces in Korea, and so on. One room devoted to Cyprus, in particular, has a virulently anti-Turkish message that seems extraordinary given current relations between the countries (it is also full of Cypriot antiquities, presumably to demonstrate the island's Greek heritage). However, the bulk of the collection consists of **weaponry and uniforms**, with a large collection of eighteenth- and nineteenth-century swords and guns, and a particular concentration on World War II. Earlier times are also covered with displays on changing warfare from Mycenae through to the Byzantines and Turks, and an array of models of the acropolises and castles of Greece, both Classical and medieval.

Outside are **artillery pieces and planes**, including a full-scale model of the Daedalus, one of the first-ever military aircraft, which dropped bombs on Turkish positions in December 1912 during the Balkan Wars.

NATIONAL ART GALLERY

Vasiléos Konstantínou 50 ⓦ www.national gallery.gr. Mon & Wed 9am–3pm & 6–9pm, Thurs–Sat 9am–3pm, Sun 10am–2pm. €6.50. MAP P.100–101, POCKET MAP H6

The **National Art Gallery** – which is combined with the private collection of Athenian lawyer Aléxandros Soútsos – holds some 9500 paintings, sculptures and engravings, as well as miniatures and furniture. Quantity, sadly, is not really matched by the quality of the exhibits.

The core collection is of **Greek art** from the sixteenth century to the present, and of the artists shown here only El Greco is well known outside Greece. One of the few modern painters to stand out is Nikos Hatzikyriakos-Ghikas (Ghika), well represented on the ground floor. On the mezzanine is a small group of canvases by the primitive painter Theophilos (more of whose work can be seen at the Museum of Greek Folk Art in Pláka; see p.41). Perhaps more interesting is the large temporary exhibition space, often hosting major travelling exhibitions; keep an eye out for posters or check in the *Athens News*.

NATIONAL ART GALLERY

Shops

BEAUTY WORKS

Kapsáli & Neofýtou Dhoúka. MAP P.100–101, POCKET MAP G6

Favoured by Madonna, this cosmetics chain, which has other branches all over Athens, stocks all the classic brands.

CAKE

Irodhótou 15. MAP P.100–101, POCKET MAP G6

Surprisingly enough, they sell cake here; not the heavy, syrupy Greek variety, but cupcakes, sponges and other home-baked goodies. Buy a slice or a whole cake to take away, or you can sit down and eat it on the spot.

DELICATESSEN

Sólonos 30. MAP P.100–101, POCKET MAP F11

Deli-supermarket that sells the likes of Marmite and chutney to desperate expats, but also has good prepared food to take away for picnics and a wide choice of local olive oil, honey and the like to take home as souvenirs.

ELENA VOTSI

Xanthoú 7. MAP P.100–101, POCKET MAP G5

An amazing little shop (not easy to find) that's home to Elena's innovative jewellery designs, which incorporate precious and semiprecious stones as well as materials such as shells. Among other things she designed the medals for the 2004 Olympics, and has worked with the likes of Gucci and Ralph Lauren.

FAVELA DRESS CODE

Skoufá 71A. MAP P.100–101, POCKET MAP F10

Youthful basement fashion boutique taking its inspiration from bright Brazilian colours.

FREE SHOP

Voukourestíou 50. MAP P.100–101, POCKET MAP F11

Upmarket contemporary boutique with own-label clothes, as well as up-and-coming Greek designers and international stalwarts like Balenciaga.

FRESH LINE

Skoufá 10. MAP P.100–101, POCKET MAP F11

Home-made bath products made from local fruits, honey, herbs, flowers and essential oils.

ICE CUBE

Tsakálof 28. MAP P.100–101, POCKET MAP F11

Beautiful designer boutique whose avant-garde designs are a welcome breath of fresh air. Attracts a young but deep-pocketed crowd. There's another branch in Glyfádha (Ioánnou Metaxá 40A).

Street markets

Weekly local street-markets are held every Friday on Xenokrátous in the heart of **Kolonáki** and on Dhragoúmi in **Ilísia**, as well as on Saturdays on Plakendías in **Ambelókipi**.

KATERINA PRASINI SHOES

Tsakálof 7. MAP P.100–101, POCKET MAP G5

A small basement shoe shop near the square where you can pick up Campers and other well-known brands, as well as bags, often at half price.

LEMISIOS

Lykavitoú 6. MAP P.100–101, POCKET MAP F11

Lemisios has been around since 1912. They mainly make leather sandals and ballet flats of a much better quality than those on sale in Pláka and Monastiráki, and can even do custom-made in two weeks: take material with you.

MARIANA PETRIDI

Háritos 34. MAP P.100–101, POCKET MAP G5

A showcase for Greek jewellery with varying styles, as well as work by Mariana Petridi herself.

TO PAIKHNIDHI

Sólonos 12. MAP P.100–101, POCKET MAP F11

Toy shop selling old-fashioned dolls, wooden toys and stuffed animals to the offspring of Athens' wealthy – at a price.

PANAYÍRI

Kleoménous 25. MAP P.100–101, POCKET MAP G5

A lovely little store selling almost nothing but model boats, mainly in the form of wall plaques, plus a few other wooden souvenirs.

PRELOVED

Asklipíou 20. MAP P.100–101, POCKET MAP F4

Vintage clothing store, usually with some interesting designer items.

THALLO

Ploútarhou 25. MAP P.100–101, POCKET MAP H5

This small jewellery shop is well worth a visit. Greek plants and flowers are coated in silver and gold to gorgeous effect and the prices are among the least intimidating in Kolonáki.

WINE GARAGE

Xenokrátous 25. MAP P.100–101, POCKET MAP H5

A trendy wine shop where the almost industrial decor is part of the attraction. That and the excellent selection of wines, both domestic and international.

Cafés

DA CAPO

Tsakálof 1. MAP P.100–101, POCKET MAP G5

A very popular establishment on this pedestrianized street, just north of Kolonáki square. *Da Capo* is very chic and, unusually, self-service.

FILION

Skoufá 34. MAP P.100–101, POCKET MAP F10

A local institution for coffee, cakes, omelettes, salads and breakfast. It's busy at all times of day, with a more sober crowd than the average Kolonáki café.

DA CAPO

FLOCAFÉ

Milióni, cnr Iraklítou. MAP P.100–101, POCKET MAP F11

Sizeable branch of this excellent café chain, hence standard prices and free wi-fi.

ROSEBUD PEOPLE'S CAFÉ BAR

Skoufá 40. MAP P.100–101, POCKET MAP F10

One of a crowd of youth-oriented café-bars around the junction of Omírou: iced coffee by day, chilled jazz/latin sounds and DJs in the first-floor bar at night. Also a restaurant serving risottos, salads and the like.

Restaurants

ALTAMIRA

Tsakálof 36A ☎ 210 36 14 695, ⓦwww .altamira.com.gr. Lunch & dinner daily. MAP P.100–101, POCKET MAP F10

Multi-ethnic menu with Mexican, Indian, Asian and Arabic dishes – on the whole well done, and an interesting change from the usual Greek fare. The setting is lovely too, upstairs in an old mansion.

BALSAMAKIS (TO KOTOPOULO)

Platía Kolonakíou 3. Lunch & dinner Mon–Sat. MAP P.100–101, POCKET MAP G5

Usually known simply as *To Kotopoulo* (the chicken), this tiny hole-in-the-wall is the place for juicy, crispy, rotisserie-style chicken, the best in Athens. It's strictly no-frills, lit by fluorescent lights and packed with people at all hours. A few tables on the pavement too, or take away to the nearby National Gardens or Lykavitós.

DHIMOKRITOS

Dhimokrítou 23 ☎ 210 36 13 588. Lunch & dinner Mon–Sat, lunch Sun; closed Aug. MAP P.100–101, POCKET MAP F10

Old-fashioned, posh and perhaps a bit snooty – lots

ALTAMIRA

of suits at lunchtime – but a beautiful building and well-prepared, reasonably priced food from a vast menu, much of which is displayed in glass counters near the entrance.

FILIPPOU

Xenokrátous 19 ☎ 210 72 16 390. Lunch & dinner Mon–Fri, lunch Sat. MAP P.100–101, POCKET MAP G5

This old-time taverna has been completely refurbished. The newly elegant interior (and a no-smoking policy that's actually enforced) hasn't changed the menu much, though; you can still check out the simmering pots and casseroles in the kitchen, or find favourites like pork in lemon sauce or rabbit with wine sauce for around €8, as well as some more ambitious, modern Greek dishes. Liveliest at lunchtime.

IKIO

Ploútarhou 15 ☎ 210 72 59 216. Lunch & dinner Mon–Sat. MAP P.100–101, POCKET MAP H5

The name means "homely", and that seems to be how the locals find it – a very busy, reasonably priced neighbourhood restaurant with a slightly modern take on Greek classics and a short menu of daily specials, plus pasta and salads.

JACKSON HALL

Milióni 4 ☎ 210 36 16 098. Daily 10am–2am. MAP P.100–101, POCKET MAP F11

A very "Kolonáki" type of place: a big, busy, expensive American-themed diner with a music bar. Burgers, steaks, pasta and salads, plus coffees and juices in the morning, cocktails and beer at night.

ORIZONTES LYCAVITOU

Summit of Lykavitós Hill ☎ 210 72 27 065. Lunch & dinner daily. MAP P.100–101, POCKET MAP G4

Fabulous views from this glassed-in eyrie, or from its sheltered terrace. The prices are just as elevated, and the complex dishes (such as sea bass with green tagliatelle and Moschato wine sauce with peanuts, at around €30) don't always live up to their promise.

OUZADIKOU

Karneádhou 25–29 ☎ 210 72 95 484. Lunch & dinner Tues–Sat. MAP P.100–101. POCKET MAP H5

An uninspiring setting in the lobby of an office building, but popular with a middle-aged Kolonáki crowd for exceptional *mezédhes*, some with a twist. Huge selection of ouzos too.

OUZERÍ

Kleoménous 22, cnr Ploútarhou, just below the funicular. Lunch & dinner daily. MAP P.100–101, POCKET MAP G5

Nameless, simply furnished and very inexpensive ouzerí with salads and sandwiches as well as good, plain *mezédhes* (small plate €4, large €7).

IL POSTINO

Grivéon 3, in alleyway off Skoufá ☎ 210 36 41 414. Lunch & dinner daily. MAP P.100–101, POCKET MAP F10

Good-value Italian trattoria, serving simple dishes in a friendly, bustling setting.

SCALA VINOTECA

Sína 50, at Anagnostopoúlou ☎ 210 36 10 041. Lunch & dinner daily. MAP P.100–101, POCKET MAP F10

Cool, architect-designed upmarket wine-bar in a minimalist modern style. The Mediterranean meze/tapas menu is delicious, and there are 100 wines to choose from. The entrance is up the steep steps at the side.

Bars

BALTHAZAR

Tsóha 27, Ambelókipi. MAP P.100–101, POCKET MAP K3

Late-night meeting place of more mature, well-heeled clubbers, *Balthazar* has a glamorous setting in an elegant mansion and its garden; restaurant earlier, cocktail bar with restrained sounds later.

CRAFT

Leofóros Alexándhras 205, Ambelókipi (by Metro Ambelókipi). MAP P.100–101, POCKET MAP K3

Vast microbrewery bar with half a dozen styles of in-house draught beer, and giant-screen TVs for entertainment. The beer brewed here is now sold right across Greece.

FRAME

Dhinokrátous 1 ☎ 210 72 14 368, Ⓦ www.frame restaurant.com. MAP P.100–101, POCKET MAP G5

Über-designer bar in the swish *St George Lycabettus Hotel*, an extraordinary amalgam of brown marble and white plastic. There are DJs and a swanky restaurant too.

MIKE'S IRISH BAR

Sinópis 6, Ambelókipi ☎ 210 77 76 797. From 9pm nightly. MAP P.100–101, POCKET MAP K4

In the shadow of the Athens Tower, this is a huge American-style basement bar with a young crowd and big screens for sporting events. Karaoke on Mondays and Tuesdays, live music most weekends.

MOMMY

Delfón 4 ☎ 210 36 19 682, ⓦ www.mommy.gr. MAP P.100–101, POCKET MAP F4

Something for everyone – a bar/café/restaurant open all day with good cocktails and fancy food (black risotto, Argentine steak). Later on, resident DJs pump out soulful house.

Clubs and live music venues

BAILA

Háritos 43 ☎ 210 72 33 019. Opens 12.30am. MAP P.100–101, POCKET MAP H5

"Freestyle" sounds in this busy club; the adjoining café-bar, *City*, offers a quieter alternative and outdoor tables.

TO BARAKI TOU VASILI

Dhidhótou 3 ☎ 210 36 23 625, ⓦ www .tobaraki.gr. From around 10.30pm, closed Sun. MAP P.100–101, POCKET MAP F10

Daily acoustic performances of Greek music: a showcase

for up-and-coming rebétika acts and popular singer-songwriters. Entry varies – around €15, including the first drink, and it's reasonably priced once you're in.

DYBBUK

Patriárkhou Ioakím 37 ☎ 210 72 21 558. Closed Sun & Mon. Typically €10 entry. MAP P.100–101, POCKET MAP G5

Glamorous basement dance club for Athens' young rich kids, frequently featuring big-name DJs.

MÉGARO MOUSIKÍS

Vassilísis Sofías at Kókkali, next to the US embassy ☎ 210 72 82 333, ⓦ www.megaron .gr. MAP P.100–101, POCKET MAP J4

Athens' premier concert hall for classical music and opera incorporates several performance spaces with great acoustics, as well as a library, restaurants and more.

PALENQUE

Farandáton 41, near Platía Ay. Thomá, Ambelókipi ☎ 210 77 52 360, ⓦ www .palenque.gr. MAP P.100–101, POCKET MAP K4

Live Latin music by South American groups, salsa parties, flamenco music and dance lessons.

Koukáki, Pangráti and Mets

South of the city centre, the neighbourhoods of Koukáki, Pangráti and Mets offer little in the way of sights, but each is full of character and home to excellent restaurants and cafés that see few tourists. Immediately south of the Acropolis and Makriyiánni, Koukáki is a plainer neighbourhood with numerous hotels and good local places to eat: even with the new Acropolis Museum nearby, hardly any visitors come here other than those who are staying. Mets, a steep hillside area on the other side of busy Syngroú avenue, is a taste of old Athens. Here a few streets of pre-World War II houses survive almost intact, their tiled roofs, shuttered windows and courtyards with spiral metal staircases and potted plants offering an intimate glimpse at the more traditional side of the city. Pangráti, nearby, has a wealth of small, homely tavernas and mezedhopolía, as well as buzzing local nightlife and good shops along Imittoú avenue.

THE PANATHENAIC STADIUM

MAP P.112, POCKET MAP G8

The old Olympic Stadium or **Panathenaic Stadium** (also dubbed Kalimármaro, "White Marble") is a nineteenth-century reconstruction on Roman foundations, slotted tightly between the pine-covered spurs of Ardhittós Hill, dividing Pangráti and Mets. You can't normally go inside, but you can go right up to the open end of its horsehoe shape, from where you get a very good view.

This site was originally marked out in the fourth century BC for the Panathenaic athletic contests, but in Roman times, as a grand gesture to mark the reign of the emperor Hadrian, it was adapted for an orgy of blood sports, with thousands of wild beasts baited

and slaughtered in the arena. The Roman senator Herodes Atticus later undertook to refurbish the 60,000 seats of the entire stadium; the white marble from these was to provide the city with a convenient quarry through the ensuing seventeen centuries.

The stadium's reconstruction dates from the modern revival of the Olympic Games in 1896 and bears witness to the efforts of another wealthy benefactor, the Alexandrian Greek Yiorgos Averoff. Its appearance – pristine whiteness and meticulous symmetry – must be very much as it was when first restored and reopened under Herodes Atticus. Though the bends are too tight for major modern events, it's still used by local athletes, is the finishing point of the annual Athens Marathon and lay at the end of the 2004 Olympic marathon.

Above the stadium to the south, on the secluded Hill of Ardhittós, are a few scant remnants of a **Temple of Fortune**, again constructed by Herodes Atticus.

SLEEPING GIRL STATUE, PRÓTO NEKROTAFÍO

THE PRÓTO NEKROTAFÍO

The **Próto Nekrotafío** (First Cemetery) shelters the tombs of just about everybody who was anybody in nineteenth- and twentieth-century Greece, from archeologist Heinrich Schliemann to actress/activist Melina Mercouri and former prime minister Andreas Papandreou. The humbler tombs of musicians, artists and writers are interspersed with ornate mausoleums of soldiers, statesmen and wealthy families, whose descendants come to picnic, stroll and tend the graves. The graveside statuary occasionally attains the status

of high art, most notably in the works of **Ianoulis Halepas**, a *belle époque* sculptor from Tínos generally acknowledged to be the greatest of a school of fellow-islanders. Halepas battled with mental illness for most of his life and died in extreme poverty in 1943; his masterpiece is the idealized *Kimiméni* (*Sleeping Girl*), on the right about 300m in.

Visiting the area

All of these areas can be reached on foot from the centre – through the Záppio Gardens to **Pangráti** or **Mets**, south from the Acropolis and Makriyiánni to **Koukáki**. If you don't fancy the stroll you can hop on a #2, #4 or #11 bus to Platía Plastíra in Pangráti or take the tram to the Panathenaic Stadium (Záppio stop); Koukáki is accessible from Akrópoli or Syngroú-Fix metro stations, or on buses #1 or #5, which run right through Makriyiánni and Koukáki.

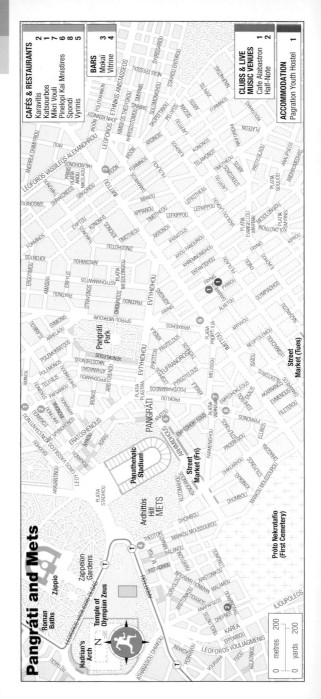

Pangráti and Mets

CAFÉS & RESTAURANTS

Karavitis	2
Katsourbos	1
Mikri Vouli	7
Pinelopi Kai Mnistires	6
Spondi	8
Vyrinis	5

BARS

Mokaï	3
Vitrine	4

CLUBS & LIVE MUSIC VENUES

Cafe Alabastron	1
Half-Note	2

ACCOMMODATION

Pagration Youth Hostel	1

Shop

TSATSOS

Veïkou 45, Koukáki. MAP P.114, POCKET MAP D8
Koukáki boasts some of the finest *zaharoplastía* (bakery/patisseries) in Athens, and Tsatsos is one of the best: try the *kadaifi* and *baklava*.

Cafés and restaurants

AMBROSIA

Dhrákou 3–5, Koukáki. ☎ 210 92 20 281.
Lunch & dinner daily. MAP P.114, POCKET MAP D9
A friendly *psistariá* (grill house) packed with locals, especially in summer when the tables spill out into the pedestrian walkway. Food is simple but delicious – grilled chicken, pork chops, kebabs and salads.

EDODI

Veïkou 80, Koukáki. ☎ 210 92 13 013.
ⓦ www.edodi.gr. Dinner only; closed Sun & July & Aug. MAP P.114, POCKET MAP C9
Some say this is the finest restaurant in Athens, and if you want to splurge on exquisitely elaborate creations in an almost theatrical atmosphere, this is the place. Starters such as lobster-tail with spinach or carpaccio of smoked goose go for €18–20, mains like sea bass with lavender or beef fillet with foie gras and truffles for around €30. Booking essential.

KARAVITIS

Arktínou 33, cnr Pafsaníou, Pangráti
☎ 210 72 15 155. Dinner only, daily, plus Sunday lunch. MAP P.112, POCKET MAP G7
This crumbling building, a lone single-storey survivor surrounded by high rises, looks unpromising, but within is a cheery old-style taverna with barrel wine, *mezédhes* and clay-cooked mains. Garden seating in summer.

KATSOURBOS

Amínta 2, Pangráti ☎ 210 72 22 167. Lunch & dinner daily. MAP P.112, POCKET MAP G7
Cretan food is highly fashionable in Athens; this modern-looking place does tasty food using ingredients sourced from the island.

MIKRI VOULI

Platía Varnáva 8, Pangráti ☎ 210 75 65 523.
Lunch & dinner daily. MAP P.112, POCKET MAP G8
A bustling *mezedhopolío* with tables on the square in summer. An excellent meze selection, and grilled meats too.

MIKRI VOULI

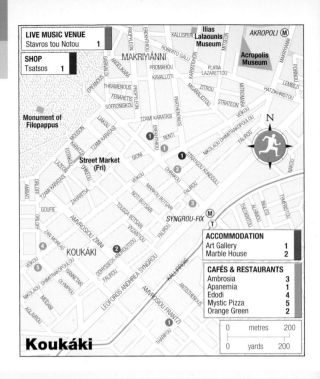

LIVE MUSIC VENUE
Stavros tou Notou 1

SHOP
Tsatsos 1

MAKRIYIÁNNI

Monument of
Filopappus

Street Market
(Fri)

KOUKÁKI

Koukáki

ACCOMMODATION
Art Gallery 1
Marble House 2

CAFÉS & RESTAURANTS
Ambrosia 3
Apanemia
Edodi 4
Mystic Pizza 5
Orange Green 2

| 0 | metres | 200 |
| 0 | yards | 200 |

MYSTIC PIZZA

Olympíou 2, Koukáki ☎ 210 95 92 092.
Weekdays 1pm–1am, weekends from 5pm.
MAP P.114, POCKET MAP C9

Cosy branch of this local chain,
serving excellent pizzas and
pastas made from flour with a
hemp (cannabis) base.

ORANGE GREEN

Dhimitrakopoúlou 42, cnr Dhrákou, Koukáki.
Daily, all day. MAP P.114, POCKET MAP D8

Huge café specializing in
home-made ice-cream; also
sandwiches, frappés and light
meals. Seating indoors and out.

PINELOPI KAI MNISTIRES

Imittoú 130 on Platía Profíti Ilía, Pangráti
☎ 210 75 68 555. Dinner Wed–Sat,
lunch & dinner Sun; closed June–Aug.
MAP P.112, POCKET MAP H8

Lively and bustling, "Penelope
and her Suitors" is a friendly,

elegant place with delicious
Greek meze as well as international dishes, plus live Greek
music from 10.30pm.

SPONDI

Pýrronos 5, Pangráti ☎ 210 75 64 021.
ⓦ www.spondi.gr. 8pm–midnight daily.
MAP P.112, POCKET MAP G8

Long-time contender for the
title of Athens' best restaurant,
Spondi has two Michelin stars
to show for the efforts of chef
Arnaud Bignon, and serves
superb French-influenced
cuisine, with fish a speciality.
With starters – crab in
herb jelly with cauliflower
mousse and Granny Smith
foam – from €34, and mains
– sea bass in mussel jam with
leek and mussels – mostly
over €40, it's not cheap, but
perfect for a special occasion.
Booking essential.

SPONDI

VYRINIS

Arhimídhous 11, Pangráti ☎ 210 70 12 153.
Lunch & dinner Mon–Sat. MAP P.112, POCKET
MAP G8

Traditional taverna redecorated in modern style (prices increased to match, so slightly above average), but still with its own house wine and some interesting *mezédhes*. Tables in a garden courtyard in summer.

Bars

MOKAÏ

Imittoú 59, Pangráti ☎ 210 75 15 345, ⓦ www.
mokaiathens.com MAP P.112, POCKET MAP J7

Busy bar/restaurant/club in the heart of Imittoú's nightlife. The bar opens around 8.30pm; later on there are regular themed party nights and DJs playing everything from hip-hop and r'n'b to 80s rock.

VITRINE

Márkou Mousoúrou 1, Mets ☎ 210 92 42 444.
Opens 9pm; closed Sun. €15 entrance Fri &
Sat. MAP P.112, POCKET MAP F14

A popular venue with the over-thirties, the balcony here has great views of Athens and Lykavitós by night. Café-bar from 9pm; later transforms into a mainstream club.

Clubs and live music venues

CAFE ALABASTRON

Damáreos 78, Pangráti ☎ 210 75 60 102,
ⓦ www.cafealavastron.gr. Closed in summer.
€6. MAP P.112, POCKET MAP H8

Excellent atmosphere and live performances of a wide variety of music, from traditional jazz to African, Latin, blues and rock. Gigs usually start around 10pm, sometimes later.

HALF-NOTE

Trivonianoú 17, Mets ☎ 210 92 13 310,
ⓦ www.halfnote.gr. Nightly at 10.30pm
(9.30pm Sun), entry €30–40 (less on Mon),
including first drink; closed much of the
summer. MAP P.112, POCKET MAP F8

Athens' premier jazz club, with live jazz, funk or rockabilly most nights and frequent big-name touring performers.

STAVROS TOU NOTOU

Tharípou 37, Neos Kosmos ☎ 210 92 26 975,
ⓦ www.stn.gr. Typically €15, including first
drink. MAP P.114, POCKET MAP D9

One of the liveliest rock clubs in town; live shows mostly feature Greek artists, but plenty of touring foreigners too.

HALF-NOTE

Around Athens

Athens sprawls higher and wider each year and most of the places covered in this chapter, originally well outside the city, are now approached through a more or less continuous urban landscape. Nonetheless, they variously offer fresh air, seaside settings, and a change of pace from downtown Athens. The coastal suburbs, from Pireás to Glyfádha, are an essential summertime escape for Athenians, who head down here in droves: not just for beaches, but for cafés, restaurants, nightlife and shops. Thanks to frequent bus and tram services it's easy to head to the beach for a quick swim and be back in the centre just a couple of hours later; astonishingly, the water almost everywhere is clean and crystal clear. Pireás, meanwhile, has ferries to the islands, an excellent museum, and some of the best seafood in town.

The inland suburb of **Kifissiá**, populated with expensive villas, provides an insight into wealthy Athenian life. Its relaxed combination of upmarket shopping and café society, especially busy on Saturdays, can be combined with a visit to the Goulandhrís Natural History Museum and Gaia Centre.

Further afield, beyond the reach of the metro and city buses, Attica (Attikí), the region encompassing the capital, is not much explored by tourists – only the great romantic ruin of the Temple of Poseidon at **Cape Soúnio** is at all well-known. Yet a trip out here makes for a pleasant break, with much of Greece in microcosm to be seen within an hour or two of the capital. There are rewarding archeological sites at **Eleusis** and **Ramnous** too,

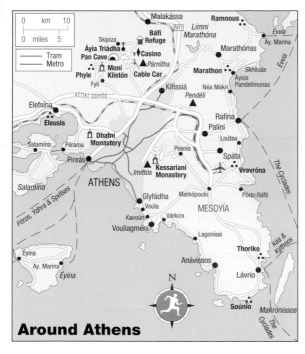

Around Athens

with plenty of **beaches** nearby. Combine these with a meal at one of the scores of seaside *psarotavernas* (fish restaurants), always packed out on summer weekends, and you've got a more than worthwhile day out.

PIREÁS

Pireás has been the port of Athens since Classical times, when the so-called Long Walls, scattered remnants of which can still be seen, were built to connect it to the city. Today

it's a substantial metropolis in its own right. The **port**, whose island ferries are the reason most visitors come here, has a gritty fascination of its own, typified by the huge Sunday-morning **flea market**, concentrated around Odhós Skilítsi, parallel to the rail tracks behind the metro station. It's not really a place to shop – the goods are mostly cheap clothing and pirated CDs, plus a few junky antiques – but it is quite an experience.

Transport to Pireás

The easiest way to **get to Pireás** from Athens is on **metro** line 1, or take the **tram** to SEF (the Stádhio Eirínis ké Fílias), which is in walking distance of Mikrolímano. **Bus** #40 (about every 10min 5am–midnight; hourly 1–5am) runs from Sýndagma, #49 from Omónia (roughly every 15min, same hours). Taxis cost about €8 at day tariff from central Athens.

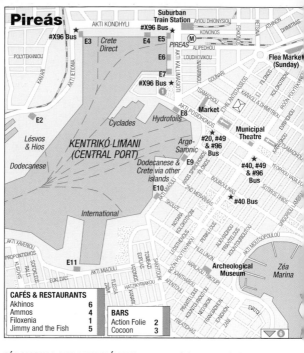

Pireás

Akti Kondhyli · #X96 Bus · #X96 Bus · E3 · Crete Direct · E4 · E5 · Suburban Train Station · Ayiou Dhionysiou · Kononos · Retsina · Athinon · Dhimitras · Polytekhniou · M · PIREÁS · Alipedhou · Ekvolis · E6 · Akti Loudhovikou · Goumari · Flea Market (Sunday) · Kanari · Akti Ietonia · E7 · #X96 Bus · Akti Kallimasioti · Tsamadhou · Ethn. Antistasseos · Karaoli & Dhimitriou · Iroon Polytekhniou · Kolokotroni · E2 · Cyclades · Market · E8 · Akti Posidhonos · Lésvos & Hios · KENTRIKÓ LIMANI (CENTRAL PORT) · Hydrofoils · Argo-Saronic · #20, #49 & #96 Bus · Municipal Theatre · Dhervenakion · Elevtheriasc · Yeoryiou Vasileos · Dodecanese · Dodecanese & Crete via other islands · Ayios Spiridhonos · E9 · #40, #49 & #96 Bus · Boubulinas · Sotiros Dhios · 2nd Merarhias · E10 · International · #40 Bus · Skouze · Kolokotroni · Leosthenous · Iroon Polytekhniou · Pedhiados · Alkiviadhou · Praxitelous · Kolokotronou · Akti Moutsopoulou · Akti Xaveriou · Propontidhos · Klisovis · Ralli · Sofokleous · Evripis · Tompazi · Kosmou · Sakhtouri · Kanthaipou · Filellmon · Haralakou Trikoupi · E11 · Akti Miaouli · Flessa · Zaim · Hatzikiriakou · Afentouli · Praxitelous · Neorion · Frangiadhon · Ydhrion · Zani · Arheological Museum · Zéa Marina · Evatou · Praxitelous · Kolyvoudhou · Filonos · Neorion · Frangiadhon · Ydhrion · Zani · Freattidhos · 6

CAFÉS & RESTAURANTS

Akhinos	6
Ammos	4
Filoxenia	1
Jimmy and the Fish	5

BARS

Action Folie	2
Cocoon	3

ZÉA MARINA AND MIKROLÍMANO

For Athenians the chief attractions of Pireás are around the small-boat harbours of **Zéa Marina** and **Mikrolímano** on the opposite side of the peninsula. Here, the upscale residential areas are alive with attractive waterfront cafés, bars and excellent fish tavernas, extremely busy at weekends. Zéa Marina (aka Pasalimáni) is worth a look to admire some of the monstrous gin palaces moored there. The boats at Mikrolímano (known to many locals as Turkolímano) are more modest than those at Zéa, but the harbour itself is prettier, and there are more cafés and restaurants to sit and enjoy it. This side of Pireás is also home to an excellent **Archeological Museum** (Hariláou Trikoúpi 31; Tues–Sun 8.30am–3pm; €3).

One of the star exhibits is a bronze *kouros* (idealized male statue) of Apollo, dating from 520–530 BC. Many other items in the museum were found at the bottom of the harbour, including the second-century AD stone reliefs of battles between Greeks and Amazons, apparently mass-produced for export to Rome.

ATHENS' BEACHES

People swim from the rocks or sea wall almost anywhere on the coast southeast of Pireás – especially the older generation (the younger ones tend to head down towards the fleshpots and pay beaches of Glyfádha) – but the closest pleasant beach to the centre is **Edem**, reached by tram to the Edem or Váthis stops. A small patch of sand with cafés and tavernas, this is busy and urban but fine for a

quick swim and, remarkably, has Blue Flag status.

There are other small, free beaches near the **Váthis** and **Flisvós** tram stops. Almost all of the really good beaches within easy reach of Athens, however, demand payment for entry. For your money you'll get clean sand, lifeguards, somewhere to buy food and drink, a lounger (usually extra) and a variety of other facilities including beach volleyball, massage, fun parks and all sorts of water sports. Some of the fanciest, in **Glyfádha** and **Vouliagméni**, charge upwards of €10 per person at weekends (the Astir Palace hotel charges an exorbitant €45); more basic places cost €3–5. There are plenty of places to swim for free, but this may mean from the rocks, or a long hike from the road. The best sandy beach with free access

is at **Skhiniás** (see box, p.124), but that's a long way out on the northeast Attic coast. On summer weekends, every beach – and the roads to them – will be packed.

Among the better pay-beaches are **Áyios Kósmas** (summer daily 9am–8.30pm; €5, children €2), a relatively quiet choice at Ag. Kosmas 2 tram stop; **Asteria** (summer daily 8am–8pm; €5, €10 weekends, children half-price), a rather glam and busy option right in the heart of Glyfádha; **Voúla A & B** (summer daily 7am–9pm; €4), large twin beaches in Voúla between Glyfádha and Vouliagméni, cheap and cheerful with decent facilities; and **Vouliagméni A** (summer daily 8am–8pm; €5), on the main road in Vouliagméni, with few facilities but a lovely setting.

GLYFÁDHA AND AROUND

Athens' southern suburbs form an almost unbroken line along the coast all the way from Pireás to Vouliagméni, some 20km away. This is the city's summer playground, and the centre of it – for shopping, clubbing, dining or posing on the beach – is **Glyfádha**, a bizarre mix of glitz and suburbia. At weekends, half of Athens seems to decamp down here. The epicentre is around the crescent of **Leofóros Angélou Metáxa**, lined with shops and malls, with the tram running down the centre and streets of cafés and restaurants heading off on either side.

Glyfádha merges almost indistinguishably into its neighbour **Voúla**, and then into quieter, more upmarket **Kavoúri** and **Vouliagméni**, one of the city's posher suburbs, whose beautiful cove beaches are a traditional hangout of Athens' rich and famous. Last stop for the local buses is **Várkiza**, more of a seaside resort pure and simple.

THE VOULIAGMÉNI PENINSULA

If you are prepared to walk a bit, or are driving and happy to battle the locals for parking space, then some of the best beaches can be found around the Vouliagméni peninsula, off the main road. Immediately after Voúla B pay beach, a road turns off to **Kavoúri**, past the *Divani Palace Hotel* and some

Transport to the beaches

For the coast as far as Glyfádha, the easiest transport option is the **tram**, and at most stops in this direction you'll be able to find somewhere to swim. For the better beaches further south, though, you'll have to take the **bus** (or transfer in Glyfádha). The main routes from central Athens are the #A2 or #E2 express (which go as far as Voúla), #A3 or #B3 (to Vouliagméni) and #E22 (all the way down the coast to Saronídha), all of which leave from Akadhimías. The #A1, #E1 and #G1 run from Pireás to Voúla. Local services #114 (Glyfádha–Kavoúri–Vouliagméni) and #115/6 (Glyfádha–Vouliagméni–Várkiza) are also useful.

If you drive, be warned that **parking** is a nightmare, especially in Glyfádha and Vouliagméni; the pay beaches all have parking, though some charge extra.

packed free beaches with excellent tavernas. Further along on this Kavoúri side of the peninsula are some still better, less crowded, free beaches: the #114 bus runs a little way inland, not far from these. Carrying on round, you get to **Vouliagméni** itself, with beautiful little coves, a few of which remain free, and eventually rejoin the main road by Vouliagméni A beach. Beyond Vouliagméni the road runs high above the coast en route to **Várkiza**; the rocky shore a steep climb below, known as Limanákia, is largely nudist and has a large gay attendance.

CAPE SOÚNIO

Aktí Souníou – **Cape Soúnio** – on the southern tip of Attica some 70km from the city centre, is one of the most imposing spots in Greece, for centuries a landmark for boats sailing between Pireás and the islands and an equally dramatic vantage-point from which to look out over the Aegean, with the Temple of Poseidon at its tip (see p.122).

Below the promontory are several **coves** – the most sheltered five minutes' walk

Soúnio transport

To get to Soúnio, take an orange KTEL Attikis **bus** from the terminal on Platía Aigiptou at the junction of Mavrommatéon and Leofóros Alexandhrás. Buses for Soúnio via the coast (€5.70; roughly 2hr) depart every hour on the half-hour from 7.30am to 5.30pm; there's also a more central (but in summer, very busy) stop ten minutes later on Filellínon, south of Sýndagma (corner of Xenofóndos). Returns are hourly on the hour from 8am to 8pm. On the less-attractive inland route to Lávrio and Soúnio there are hourly departures from 5.45am to 8.45pm, returning on the half-hour.

east from the car park and site entrance. The main **Soúnio beach**, a short distance to the north, is more crowded, but has a couple of tavernas at the far end. The port of **Lávrio**, a little further round the coast, has numerous cafés and restaurants, as well as a one-room **Archeological Museum** (Tues–Sun 10am–3pm; €2) with finds from the site.

THE TEMPLE OF POSEIDON

Daily 9.30am–sunset; €4.

The captivating fifth-century-BC **Temple of Poseidon**, built in the time of Pericles as part of a major sanctuary to the sea god, is now in a picturesque state of semi-ruin. The temple owes much of its fame to **Byron**, who visited in 1810, carved his name on the nearest pillar (an unfortunate and much-copied precedent) and immortalized the place in verse:

Place me on Sunium's marbled steep,
Where nothing, save the waves and I,
May hear our mutual murmurs sweep;
There, swan-like, let me sing and die:
A land of slaves shall ne'er be mine –
Dash down yon cup of Samian wine!

from *Don Juan*

In summer, at least, there is faint hope of silent solitude, unless you slip into the site before the tour groups arrive or after they've left. Despite this, the setting is still wonderful – on a clear day, the **view** takes in the islands of Kéa, Kýthnos and Sérifos to the southeast, Égina and the Peloponnese to the west – and the temple as evocative a ruin as any in Greece. Doric in style, it was probably built by the architect of the Hephaisteion in the Athens Agora.

The rest of the site is of more academic interest. There are remains of a fortification wall around the sanctuary; a *propylaion* (entrance hall) and stoa; cuttings for two shipsheds; and the foundations of a small Temple of Athena.

KIFISSIÁ

Set on the leafy lower slopes of Mount Pendéli, about 10km north of the city centre at the end of Metro line 1, **Kifissiá** is one of Athens' swishest suburbs. In the nineteenth century the area began to develop as a bourgeois summer residence, cooler and healthier than the city centre. The original villas – Neoclassical, Swiss or simply vulgar – still hold their own amid the newer concrete models. The metro and downtown pollution helped accelerate development, but Kifissiá is still distinctly "old money", despite the fact that these days it has a thoroughly suburban atmosphere, and the local branches of Gucci and Chanel are housed in upmarket malls.

Still, it's a fascinating place to see how the other half lives, full of pricey cafés and bars where young locals preen and gossip on their mobiles.

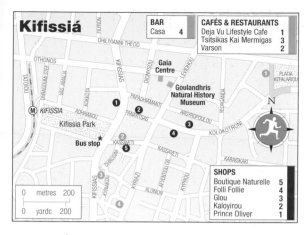

Kifissiá

BAR	
Casa	4

CAFÉS & RESTAURANTS	
Deja Vu Lifestyle Cafe	1
Tsitsikas Kai Mermigas	3
Varson	2

SHOPS	
Boutique Naturelle	5
Folli Follie	4
Glou	3
Kaloyirou	2
Prince Oliver	1

GOULANDHRÍS NATURAL HISTORY MUSEUM

Levidhou 13 🌐 www.gnhm.gr. Tues–Sat 9am–2.30pm, Sun 10am–2.30pm. €5.

Set in a fine old mansion, the **Goulandhrís Natural History Museum** has especially good coverage of Greek birds, butterflies, and endangered species like the monk seal and loggerhead sea-turtle, plus a 250,000-specimen herbarium. Perhaps more interesting, especially for kids, the **Gaia Centre** (same hours; €5), with its own entrance round the corner at Óthonos 100, offers a mildly interactive trip through the natural cycle of the earth and ecological issues. Labelling is in Greek only, but audio guides are available in English. The museum has a **café** and a **shop** selling superb illustrated books, postcards, posters and prints.

RAFÍNA

The east coast is a favourite weekend and holiday escape for jaded Athenians, many of whom have second homes out here. The main route out of the city leads straight for the little port of **Rafína**, from where you can head off to numerous islands, including nearby Évvia. Boats aside, the appeal of the place is mainly gastronomic: overlooking the harbour is a line of excellent seafood restaurants, many with a ringside view of the comings and goings of the port.

WATERFRONT TAVERNAS, RAFÍNA

East-coast transport

There are **buses** to Rafína (40min) and to Marathónas (many via the beaches at Skhiniás) every 30 minutes throughout the day from the KTEL Attikis terminal on Mavrommatéon. Ramnous is not realistically accessible by public transport. **By car**, the main route is straight out on Messoyíon (following airport signs) onto the eastbound Leofóros Marathónos, which heads straight for Rafína and Marathon.

MARATHON AND AROUND

The site of the **battle of Marathon**, the most famous and arguably most important military victory in Athenian history, is not far north of Rafína; the burial mound of the Athenian dead, the **Týmfos Marathóna** (Tues–Sun 8.30am–3pm; €3), can still be seen, off the main road between Rafína and Marathónas village.

The coast around Marathon has some great stretches of sand. **Áyios Pandelímonas**, also known as Paralía Marathónas, is straight on past the burial mound. The beach here is small, but a string of excellent waterfront fish-tavernas ensure plenty of local visitors in summer. There's a far better beach to the north at **Skhiniás**, a long, pine-backed strand with shallow water, big enough to allow some chance of escaping the crowds.

RAMNOUS

Daily: summer 8am–5.30pm, winter 8.30am–3pm. €2.

The little-visited ruins of **Ramnous** occupy an isolated, atmospheric site above the sea, with magnificent views across the strait to Évvia. The site was an Athenian lookout point from the earliest times, and remains of walls and fortifications can clearly be seen continuing way below the fenced site, all the way down to the rocky shore.

Within the site, the principal ruin is a Doric **Temple of Nemesis**, goddess of divine retribution. Pausanias records that the Persians incurred the wrath of the goddess by

The Mysteries of Eleusis

The ancient **Mysteries** had an effect on their initiates that was easily the equal of any modern cult. Established in Mycenaean times, perhaps as early as 1500 BC, the cult centred on **Demeter**, the goddess of corn, and her daughter **Persephone**'s annual descent into and resurrection from the underworld, which came to symbolize the rebirth of the crops and the miracle of fertility. By the fifth century BC the cult had developed into a sophisticated annual festival, attracting up to 30,000 people every autumn. The ceremonies lasted nine days: the **Sacred Objects** (identity unknown) were taken to Athens, where they were stored in the Ancient Agora. Various rituals took place in the city before finally a vast procession brought the objects back, following the Sacred Way to the sanctuary at **Eleusis**. Here initiates took part in the final rituals of legomena (things said), dhromena (things done) and dheiknumena (things shown). One theory suggests that these rituals involved drinking a fungus-infused potion, producing similar effects to those of modern psychedelic drugs.

their presumption in bringing with them to Greece a giant marble block upon which they intended to commemorate their victory. They met their nemesis, however, at the battle of Marathon, and the Athenians used the marble to create a statue instead.

ELEUSIS (ELEFSÍNA)

Tues–Sun: summer 8am–7pm, winter 8.30am–3pm. €3.

The **Sanctuary of Demeter** at **Eleusis**, on the edge of the modern town of Elefsína, was one of the most important in the ancient Greek world. For two millennia, the ritual ceremonies known as the Mysteries (see box, opposite) were performed here. Today, the extensive ruins of the sanctuary occupy a low hill on the coast in the heart of modern Elefsína's industrial blight. The site offers something of an escape from its surroundings: from outside the museum, at one of the highest points, the

gulf and its rusty shipping even manage to look attractive.

The best plan on arrival is to head straight for the **museum**, which features models of the sanctuary at various stages in its history: Eleusis is impressively large, with huge walls and gates, some of which date back to Mycenaean times, but the numerous eras of building can also be confusing, especially as signage is poor and mainly in Greek. As well as the models and maps, the museum has some excellent finds from the site, especially **Roman statuary**. Exploring outside, the most important structure of ancient Eleusis was the **Telesterion**. This windowless Hall of Initiation lay at the heart of the cult, and it was here that the priests of Demeter would exhibit the Sacred Objects and speak "the Unutterable Words".

City **buses** #A16, #B16 or express #E16 run frequently from Platía Eleftherías in central Athens to Elefsína.

Shops

BOOM

Platía Katráki 1, Glyfádha.

Right on the main square at the entrance to Glyfádha, this is a large, multi-brand discount fashion store on three huge floors with an all-day café-bar.

BOUTIQUE NATURELLE

Kassavéti 4, Kifissiá. MAP P.123

Handmade cosmetics and soaps at competitive prices.

BSB

Angélou Metáxa 40, cnr Fívis, Glyfádha.

Greek fashion label that makes an interesting alternative to the well-known names all around.

FOLLI FOLLIE

Angélou Metáxa 8, Glyfádha; Koloktróni 8, Kifissiá. MAP P.123

Home turf for this Athens-based jewellery, watch and accessory chain that now has a worldwide presence.

GLOU

Koloktróni 6, Kifissiá. MAP P.123

In the very heart of the Kifissiá shopping area, this reasonably priced Greek men's fashion chain has its own fashion range, as well as stocking designer sportswear.

KALOYIROU

Panayítsas 4A, Kifissiá. MAP P.123

This high-class, long-established shoe store sells its own designs, plus international brands too.

LAK

Angélou Metáxa 24–26, Glyfádha.

Tiny place featuring designer clothes for well-heeled and super-trendy youngsters.

PRINCE OLIVER

Lazaráki 35, Glyfádha; Kifisías 242 cnr Panayítsas, Kifissiá. MAP P.123

Greek men's fashion chain with a wide selection of formal and casual gear.

Cafés

COSI

Zissimopoúlo 12, Glyfádha.

This is just one of a crowd of glam, upmarket café-bars on this street just off the main shopping drag in the heart of chichi Glyfádha.

DÉJA VU LIFESTYLE CAFÉ

Platía Kefalaríou, Kifissiá. MAP P.123

The name says it all – this is the place to to see and be seen while lingering over your cappuccino freddo or salad lunch.

FILOXENIA

Aktí Tsélegi 4, Pireás. MAP P.118–119

Less manic than most places around the port, with tables outside on a pedestrianized part of the waterfront just off Platía Karaïskáki, this café serves breakfast and light meals throughout the day. Handy if you're waiting for a ferry.

PAGOTO MANÍA

Konstantinoupoléos 5, Glyfádha.

Wonderful ice cream in a huge variety of flavours, plus all the usual café fare.

VARSON

Kassavéti 5, Kifissiá. MAP P.123

This huge, old-fashioned café/patisserie is an Athens institution. Home-made yoghurts, jams and sticky cakes to take away or to enjoy with a coffee in the cavernous interior or in a quiet courtyard out back.

AMMOS

Restaurants

AKHINÓS

Aktí Themistokléous 51, Pireás
☎ 210 45 26 944. Lunch & dinner Tues–Sun.
MAP P.118–119

This place serves wonderful
seafood and Greek specialities on a covered terrace
overlooking a beach. The fish
is pricey, but less so than the
harbourfront alternatives. Book
at weekends.

AKRIOYIALI

Soúnio beach, by the Aegeon hotel
☎ 229 20 39 107. Lunch & dinner daily in
summer, lunch only Oct–April.

Simple beachside taverna with
both character and history – a
number of illustrious Greeks
have dined here. The food,
mainly fish, is simple but
cooked to perfection.

AKTI

Possidhónos 6, Vouliagméni ☎ 210 89 60 448.
Lunch & dinner daily.

On the main road just beyond
the Vouliagméni peninsula,
with waterfront tables and
great views, this is a top-class
fish taverna. Fish is expensive
and so is Vouliagméni; by those
standards €50–60 for a main is
decent value. Booking is essential for the waterfront tables.

AMMOS

Aktí Koumoundhoúrou 44, Mikrolímano,
Pireás ☎ 210 42 24 633. Lunch & dinner
daily. MAP P.118–119

In contrast to the high-luxe
places surrounding it, *Ammos*
goes for an island feel, with
hand-painted tables and beach
scenes. Mainly fish, but a wide
variety of meze, and slightly
lower prices and a younger
crowd than its neighbours.

BUFFALO BILL'S

Kýprou 13, Glyfádha ☎ 210 89 43 128. Dinner
Mon–Sat, lunch & dinner Sun.

Get into the Glyfádha mood
at this lively Tex-Mex joint.
As you'd expect, there are
tacos, steaks and chilli, plus
margaritas by the jugful.

GEORGE'S STEAK HOUSE

Konstantinoupóleos 4, Glyfádha
☎ 210 894 6020. Lunch & dinner daily.

Despite the name, this is a
traditional Greek grill-house,
large, reasonably priced and
very popular. The menu
includes excellent lamb chops
and meatballs. Located on
a side-street crowded with
restaurants close to the main
Platía Katráki tram stop.

GEORGE'S STEAK HOUSE

ISLAND

Limanákia Vouliagménis, km27 on Athens–Soúnio road between Vouliagméni and Várkiza ☎ 210 96 53 563, Ⓦ www.islandclub restaurant.gr. Summer only, daily 9.30pm till late (club from 11pm).

Beautiful bar/restaurant/club with a breathtaking clifftop setting which, as the name suggests, evokes island life. It's very chic and not as expensive as you might expect at €15–25 for a main course, with modern Mediterranean food and a tapas lounge. Booking essential. See also opposite.

JIMMY AND THE FISH

Aktí Koumoundhoúrou 46, Mikrolímano, Pireás ☎ 210 41 24 417, Ⓦ www.jimmyandthefish.com Daily midday–2am. MAP P.118–119

Excellent, glamorous and inevitably expensive fish-taverna occupying the prime position among the harbourside places on Mikrolímano. Booking essential at weekends.

TA KAVOÚRIA TOU ASIMÁKI

Limáni, Rafína ☎ 229 40 24 551. Lunch & dinner daily.

The first of the harbourside tavernas as you walk down

JIMMY AND THE FISH

from town, and arguably the best, with a fine view from its rooftop tables. Fish is the inevitable speciality, but plenty of other choice too.

OUZERI LIMENI

Platía Plastíra 17, Rafína ☎ 229 40 24 750. Lunch & dinner: closed Sun & Mon in winter.

One of several options on the pedestrianized square above the harbour, *Limeni* serves excellent, inexpensive meze.

SYRTAKI

Near Soúnio, on road towards Lávrio ☎ 229 20 39 125. Fri–Sun lunch & dinner, plus some weekdays in summer.

Popular place serving standard taverna fare, including seafood at reasonable prices.

TRIA ADHELFIA

Paralía Marathónas, 300m north of Marathónas ☎ 229 40 56 461. Fri–Sun dinner & Sun lunch, plus weekdays in summer.

Simple seafood taverna with a stunning waterfront position.

TSITSIKAS KAI MERMIGAS

Dhrosíni 12, Kifissiá ☎ 210 62 30 080. Lunch & dinner Mon–Sat. MAP P.123

One of a small chain of popular Athenian restaurants,

TA KAVOÚRIA TOU ASIMÁKI

the "Ant and the Grasshopper" is designed to look something like a traditional village store, serving Greek dishes with a modern twist. Mostly, in dishes like kid with rosemary and *raki*, it works well, though some of the more elaborate combinations can fall flat. Great ambience, and always busy.

VINCENZO

Yiannitsopoúlou 1, Glyfádha ☎ 210 89 41 310. Lunch & dinner daily.
Good, reasonably priced Italian fare, including excellent pizzas from a wood-fired oven.

Bars

ACTION FOLIE

Aktí Dhilavéri 9–11, Mikrolímano, Pireás. MAP P.118–119
Café-bar that's open all day and most of the night, every day. The tables outside make a good place to check out all the action of this buzzing nightlife area, and there's funky music too.

CASA

Platía Ayíou Dhimítriou 13, Kifissiá. MAP P.123
Attractive bar/café/restaurant, beautifully set in a blue-and-white mansion on a quiet Kifissiá square.

COCOON

Aktí Koumoundoúrou, Mikrolímano, Pireás. MAP P.118–119
There are dozens of bars and cafés around Mikrolímano and along the coast to the east. This is one of the biggest, with an ambience that ranges from waterfront lounging over coffee by day to early-hours clubbing.

MOLLY MALONE'S

Yiannitsopoúlou 8, Glyfádha ☎ 210 89 44 247.
Irish-run pub offering a warm welcome, cold Guinness and a distinctively Irish-Greek *craic*. Good food too, from sandwiches to steaks to Irish stew.

Clubs

AMMOS BEACH

Loutrá Alímou, off Possidhónos ☎ 210 98 55 848. Entry from €10, including first drink.
On the seafront between Pireás and Glyfádha, at Loutrá Alímou tram stop, *Ammos Beach* lives up to its name, with an excellent beach. At night there are parties and themed events, plus Greek and international DJs, with predominantly R&B and house music.

BALUX

Possidhónos 58, Glyfádha ☎ 210 89 41 620. Summer only. Entry from €15, including first drink.
On Astéras beach in the heart of Glyfádha, *Balux* attracts a hip, moneyed, young crowd. The music may be anything from hip-hop to 80s disco. The complex also includes a pool, and a daytime café.

CANDY BAR SUMMER PARADISE

Possidhónos, right by Áyios Kósmas beach ☎ 210 33 17 801. Summer only. Entry from €15, including first drink.
Big, happening place with a variety of club nights and events; Greek music on Wednesdays, r'n'b Thursdays, plus big-name DJs at weekends.

ISLAND

Limanákia Vouliagménis, km27 on Athens–Soúnio road between Vouliagméni and Várkiza ☎ 210 96 53 563, ☎ www.island clubrestaurant.gr. Summer only, from 11pm.
Stunning clifftop setting attracts a chic, stylish crowd. One way to be sure of making it past the queue and the bouncers is to book into the restaurant (see opposite).

Further afield

With the use of a hire car or by taking one of the many tours available, you can visit a wealth of sites and attractions within a few hours of Athens. Highlights include the stunning ruins of Delphi (site of the famous Delphic Oracle), mountain hiking on the slopes of Mount Parnassós and the impressive ancient sites of Tiryns and Mycenae. From the port of Pireás, too, you can easily jump on a ferry or hydrofoil and be on a Greek island in the Argo-Saronic gulf within an hour or two, making for some wonderfully varied day-trips – although, with countless places to stay everywhere you go, you might be tempted to stay longer.

MOUNT PARNASSÓS

Rising to almost 2500 metres at its highest point, **Mount Parnassós** is a popular climbing and walking destination, as well as a ski and snowboard centre in winter. In its shadow crouch Delphi and the mountain village of Aráhova. The heights are easily accessible, and though they no longer rank as complete wilderness, thanks to the ski station above Aráhova and its

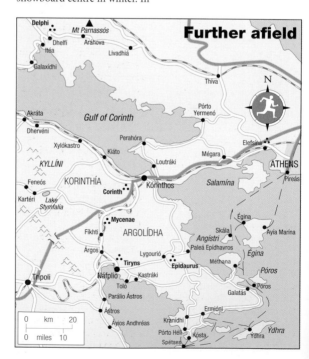

ARÁHOVA

accompanying lifts, snack bars and access roads, the area still provides an attractive break from the city.

There are plenty of good **walks**, ranging from challenging all-day climbs to numerous short trails. With your own transport you could drive up the mountain from Aráhova to the south, or from Lílea, Polýdhrosos or Amfília on the north slope, any of which can be combined with a walk. The best of the major hikes is the return journey from Dhelfí to the Corycian cave; about four hours up, slightly less down. This is practicable from April to November, but not in midsummer without a dawn start; an easier alternative is to get a taxi up to the cave and walk down. Well-signed as part of the E4 path, the route can make a fair claim to being one of the longest-used footpaths on the planet, having been trodden since the earliest times as a route to the cave, where Pan was worshipped. Another challenging route takes you from the Yerondóvrakhos ski station to the mountain's main summit, Liákoura (2457m; May–Oct only).

ARÁHOVA

The strung-out village of **Aráhova**, dwarfed by the peaks of Parnassós, is a picturesque little place, with its vernacular architecture, stone walls, wooden eaves, and shops selling all kinds of arts, crafts and foodstuffs. During the winter it's popular with skiers, but it's worth a brief stop at any time of year to browse the wide variety of local produce – including wine, cheese and the local pasta known as *hilópittes* – and to wander the attractive backstreets that wind off the busy main road. There are plenty of good restaurants, many distinctly upmarket; not all are open in summer, however.

The local **festival of Áyios Yeóryios** (April 23, or the Tuesday after Easter if this date falls within Lent), centred on the church at the top of the hill, is the excuse for almost two days of continuous partying, and one of the best opportunities in the region to see authentic folk-dancing.

Buses between Athens and Delphi (see p.133) stop in Aráhova, half an hour from Delphi.

The Delphic Oracle

The origins of the **Oracle at Delphi** are uncertain, but certainly by the ninth century BC there was a thriving sanctuary here, dedicated to Apollo. For over a thousand years thereafter, a steady stream of pilgrims made its way up the dangerous mountain paths to seek divine direction in matters of war, worship, love or business. On arrival they would pay a set fee, sacrifice a goat, boar or even a bull and, depending on the omens, wait to submit questions inscribed on lead tablets. The priestess, a simple and devout village woman of fifty or more years in age, would chant her prophecies from a tripod positioned over the oracular chasm and an attendant priest would then "interpret" her utterances in verse.

Many of the answers were equivocal at best. King Croesus of Lydia, for example, was told that if he embarked on war against neighbouring Persia he would destroy a mighty empire; he did – his own. But it's hard to imagine that the oracle would have retained its popularity and influence for so long without offering predominantly sound advice.

DELPHI

Sacred Precinct daily: summer 7.30am–7.30pm; winter 8.30am–3pm. Museum same hours except Mon in summer 12.30–6pm. €9

Perched on the slopes of a high mountain terrace and dwarfed to either side by the massive crags of Mount Parnassós, it's easy to see why the ancients believed **Delphi** to be the centre of the earth. As if the natural setting and occasional earthquake and avalanche weren't enough to confirm a divine presence, this, according to Plutarch, was where a rock chasm was discovered that exuded strange vapours and reduced people to frenzied, incoherent and prophetic mutterings. Thus was born the famous **Delphic Oracle** (see box above), to which kings and simple citizens flocked in an attempt to foresee the future.

Delphi is a large and complex ruin, best taken in two stages, with the sanctuary and precinct ideally at the beginning or end of the day, or (in winter) at lunchtime, to escape the crowds.

THE THOLOS AT DELPHI

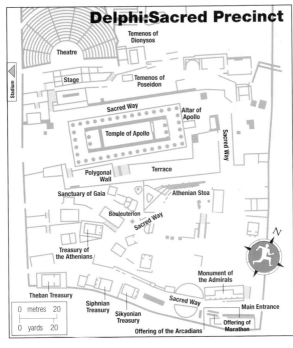

Delphi:Sacred Precinct

Temenos of Dionysos

Theatre

Temenos of Poseidon

Stage

Stadium

Sacred Way

Altar of Apollo

Temple of Apollo

Sacred Way

Polygonal Wall

Terrace

Sanctuary of Gaia

Athenian Stoa

Bouleuterion

Sacred Way

Treasury of the Athenians

Monument of the Admirals

Theban Treasury

Siphnian Treasury

Sacred Way

Main Entrance

Sikyonian Treasury

Offering of Marathon

Offering of the Arcadians

N

0 metres 20

0 yards 20

The **Sacred Precinct** contains most of the sights – including the Temple of Apollo, the impressive theatre and the stadium – but Delphi's most iconic building, the fourth-century-BC **Tholos**, is found in the **Marmaria**, or Sanctuary of Athena, ten minute' walk along the main road. The structure has been partly reconstructed, amply demonstrating its original beauty, though its purpose remains a mystery. The historic **Castalian spring**, located on a sharp bend between the Marmaria and the Sacred Precinct, is marked by niches for votive offerings and by the remains of an archaic fountain-house – water still flows from a cleft in the Phaedriades cliffs.

Modern **Dhelfí**, just west of the site, is almost entirely geared to tourism, with easy access to the site and Mount Parnassós. The tourist office (Mon–Fri 8am–2.30pm; ☎ 226 50 82 900) is in the town hall.

Up to six **buses** a day run to Delphi from Athens, leaving from the Liossíon terminal (3hr). By **car**, take the old road towards Thebes.

TEMPLE OF APOLLO, DELPHI

ANCIENT CORINTH

Daily: summer 8.30am–7pm, winter 8am–5pm.
€6; Acrocorinth free.

The ruins of **ancient Corinth**, an important city throughout the Classical era and the most powerful in Greece in Roman times, occupy a rambling sequence of sites that encompass sections of ancient walls, outlying stadiums, gymnasiums and necropolises. The highlight here is the majestic ruin of the **Temple of Apollo**, a fifth-century-BC survivor of the Classical era. Still more compelling, though, are the ruins of the medieval city, which occupy the stunning acropolis of **Acrocorinth**, towering 565m above the ancient city on an enormous mass of rock, still largely encircled by two kilometres of wall. This became one of Greece's most powerful fortresses during the Middle Ages.

There's a four-kilometre climb to the entrance gate (an hour's walk, or taxis are usually available at ancient Corinth), but it's worth it: from the top, overlooking the Saronic and Corinthian gulfs, you really get a sense of the site's strategic importance. Amid the extensive remains, you wander through a jumble of chapels, mosques, houses and battlements, erected in turn by Greeks, Romans, Byzantines, Frankish crusaders, Venetians and Turks.

Modern Kórinthos is easily accessible from Athens by **bus** (very frequently from the terminal at Kifissoú 100; 1hr 30min), road or fast suburban rail, and there are buses to the ancient site at least hourly from there, and plenty of taxis.

EPIDAURUS

Site: summer daily 8am–7pm, winter 8am–5pm; museum: same hours but opens noon on Mon. €6 joint ticket.

Epidaurus (Epídhavros) is visited primarily for its stunning **ancient theatre**, built around 330–320 BC, whose setting makes a compelling venue for productions of Classical drama as part of the annual Athens Festival (see p.158). With its backdrop of rolling hills, the 14,000-seat theatre merges perfectly into the landscape – so well, in fact, that it was rediscovered only in the nineteenth century. Constructed with mathematical precision, it has near-perfect acoustics – such that you can hear coins, or even matches, dropped in the circular

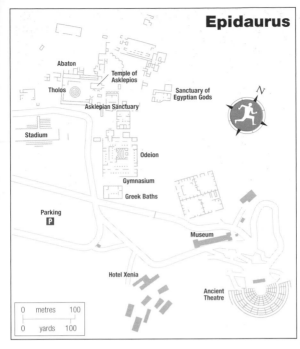

Epidaurus

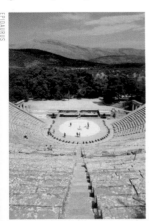

orchestra from the highest of the 54 tiers of seats.

The theatre, however, is just one component of what was one of the most important sanctuaries in the ancient world, dedicated to the healing god Asklepios. A place of pilgrimage for half a millennium, from the sixth century BC into Roman times, it's now a World Heritage site.

Close by the theatre is a small **museum**, which is best visited before you explore the rest of the sanctuary – most of the ruins visible today are just foundations, so dropping in here helps identify some of the former buildings. The finds displayed show the progression of medical skills and cures used at the Asklepion; there are tablets recording miraculous cures alongside advanced-looking surgical instruments.

For festival performances, special **buses and boats** run to Epidaurus from both Athens and Náfplio. Otherwise there are two buses daily from Athens (2hr 30min), and four from Náfplio (30min), plus an array of tours.

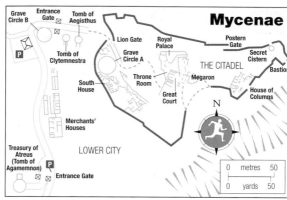

MYCENAE

Summer Mon–Fri 8am–7pm, Sat & Sun 8.30am–5pm; winter Mon–Fri 8am–5pm, Sat & Sun 8.30am–3pm; museum opens at noon on Mon. €8.

Tucked into a fold of the hills just east of the road from Kórinthos to Árgos, the citadel at **Mycenae** (Mykínes) bears testament above all to the obsession of the archeologist Heinrich Schliemann with proving that the tales of Homer had their basis in fact (see box, below).

The extensive site is made up of two parts – the citadel itself and the Treasury of Atreus. The most visually arresting part of the citadel is the **Lion Gate**, whose huge sloping gateposts and walls were considered Cyclopean by later Greeks, who could only imagine that a Cyclops could have constructed them. Beyond, the impressive **Grave Circle** known as "A" was originally thought by Schliemann to be the actual tomb of Agamemnon, though it subsequently proved to be hundreds of years too old for that. It was here that the famous gold death-mask, now in the National Archeological Museum (see p.89), was found in 1876. The rest of the site is scattered over the hillside, while just down the road is the tremendously impressive **Treasury of Atreus**, now described as the **Tomb of Agamemnon**. This was

Agamemnon, Homer and the discovery of Mycenae

In the tales related in Homer's Iliad and Odyssey, **Agamemnon** was the commander of the Greek forces in the Trojan War; a war that started when **Paris**, son of the king of Troy, abducted **Helen**, wife of Menelaus, king of Sparta and brother to Agamemnon. Homer's "well-built Mycenae, rich in gold" was the most powerful city in Greece at the time. Its rulers, though, lived under a curse from the gods that saw Agamemnon sacrifice his own daughter, Iphigenia, and then, on his return from the war, be murdered in his bath by his wife, Klytemnestra, and her lover. Until the late nineteenth century, all this was thought to be mere myth. But then German archeologist **Heinrich Schliemann** discovered, first, the site of Troy and then, in 1874, Mycenae itself.

LION GATE, MYCENAE

certainly a royal burial vault at a late stage in Mycenae's history, so the attribution to Agamemnon or his father is as good as any. Whoever it might have belonged to, this beehive-like structure is an impressive monument to Mycenaean building skills.

Buses between Náfplio and Athens (see Náfplio) will drop you about ten minutes' walk from the site, or there are regular local buses from Náfplio.

TIRYNS

Daily: summer 8am–7pm, winter 8.30am–3pm. €3.

In Mycenaean times the ancient fortress of **Tiryns** (Tíryntha) commanded the coastal approaches to Árgos and Mycenae. The Aegean shore, however, gradually receded, leaving this impressive structure stranded on a low hillock in today's plains, surrounded by citrus groves, alongside a large modern prison. The setting is less impressive than that of its showy neighbour Mycenae, which in part explains why this highly accessible, substantial site is relatively empty of visitors; the opportunity to wander

about Homer's "wall-girt Tiryns" in near-solitude is worth taking. The site lies just off the main Árgos–Náfplio road, and half-hourly local **buses** from Náfplio stop outside.

NÁFPLIO

A lively, beautifully sited seaside town, **Náfplio** exudes a grand, slightly faded elegance, inherited from the days when it was the fledgling capital of modern Greece in the early nineteenth century. The postcard-pretty old town, with its paved and mostly pedestrianized streets, is full of colourful restaurants and craft shops, and there's a pleasant buzz that you don't often witness in Greek towns.

Café life – swelled at weekends by crowds of Athenians – reaches the heights of urban chic in the cafés lining the palm-tree-fringed seafront of Bouboulínas. Things are quieter on Platía Syndágmatos, where places stay open late.

For the fit, the climb up to the twin fortresses of **Palamídhi** (daily: summer 8am–7pm, winter 8am–6.30pm; €4), out on the headland overlooking the old town, is well worth the effort. The town's third fort, the stunning **Boúrtzi**, occupies the Ayíou Theodhórou islet offshore from the harbour, and was built in 1473 by the Venetians to control the shipping lane to the town and to much of Árgos bay.

You can get to Náfplio by **bus** (from Kifissoú 100; 2hr) or – much slower but much more attractive – by **train** via Corinth (where you have to change). Both bus and train stations are within 500m of the old town precinct.

Island transport

Angístri, Égina, Póros and Ýdhra are served by a minimum of six hydrofoils daily (more at busy times) from Pireás. It's wise to book at weekends and busy summer periods; otherwise just turn up at the port (between gates E8 and E9). Regular **ferries** – cheaper but slower – also go to Égina and Póros. Schedules and online booking at ⓦ www.hellenic seaways.gr and ⓦ www.aegeanflying dolphins.gr.

ÉGINA

A substantial and attractive island with a proud history, less than an hour from Pireás, **Égina** is not surprisingly a popular weekend escape from Athens. Despite the holiday homes, it retains a laidback, island atmosphere, especially if you visit midweek or out of season. Famous for its **pistachio orchards** – the nuts are hawked from stalls all around the harbour – the island can also boast substantial ancient remains, the finest of which is the beautiful fifth-century BC **Temple of Aphaea** (summer daily 8am–7pm, winter Tues–Sun 8am–5pm; €4), commanding superb views towards Athens from high above the northeast coast, close to the resort and port of **Ayía Marína** (also accessible by direct boat from Pireás).

Égina Town, the island's capital, boasts grand old buildings around a large, busy harbour. The Neoclassical architecture is matched by a sophisticated ethos: by island standards this is a large town, with plenty of shopping, a well-stocked bazaar which remains lively even at weekends, a semi-permanent yacht-dwelling contingent and no shortage of attractive places to eat and drink. The low-key fishing village of **Pérdhika**, scenically set on a little bay packed with yachts, is also worth a visit.

Local **buses** run to all of Égina's sights, or you can rent a scooter.

ANGÍSTRI

Angístri, just fifteen minutes by fast boat from Égina, is a tiny island, obscure enough to be overlooked by most island-hoppers. There's a small, not terribly attractive strip of development on the north coast, facing Égina, but the rest of the island is pine-covered, timeless and beautiful – albeit with very few beaches. It's also strangely schizophrenic: holiday weekends can see hordes of young Greeks camping out on otherwise empty beaches, while in the port at **Skála** a few small, classy hotels are juxtaposed with cafés serving English breakfasts to package trippers.

The secluded, pebbly beach at **Halikádha**, a short walk around the rocks from Skála, is almost deserted except on summer weekends, and predominantly nudist. The slightly scary scramble down the cliffs is rewarded by the island's best swimming.

PÓROS

Separated from the mainland by a 350-metre strait, **Póros** ("the ford") barely qualifies as an island at all. More than its neighbours, Póros attracts holiday-makers as well as weekending Athenians, who can get here easily by road (via Galatás). There are in fact two islands, Sferiá (Póros Town) and the far larger **Kalávria**, separated from each other by a miniature canal, spanned by a bridge. Longer-term visitors base themselves on Kalávria, where several good beaches are easily reached on the local bus.

Póros Town itself is a busy place, with constant traffic of shipping and people: a place to eat, drink, shop and watch the world go by. Away from the waterfront you'll quickly get lost in the labyrinth of steep, narrow streets, but nowhere is far away and most of the restaurants well signed. For a fine view over the rooftops and the strait, climb up to the clock tower.

ÝDHRA (HYDRA)

The island of **Ýdhra** is one of the most atmospheric and refreshing destinations in Greece. Its harbour and main town preserved as a national monument, it feels like a Greek island should, entirely traffic-free (even bicycles are banned), with a bustling harbour and narrow stone streets climbing steeply above it. Away from the main settlement, the rest of the island is roadless, rugged and barely inhabited. The charm

hasn't gone unnoticed – Ýdhra became fashionable as early as the 1950s – but even the seasonal and weekend crowds can't seriously detract from its appeal. When the town is over-run, it's easy enough to leave it all behind on foot or by excursion boat.

The **port**, with tiers of substantial grey-stone mansions and humbler white-walled, red-tiled houses rising from a perfect horseshoe harbour, forms a beautiful spectacle. The waterfront mansions were built mostly during the eighteenth century on the wealth of a merchant fleet which traded as far afield as America. Fortunes were made and the island attracted immigrants from the less privileged mainland; by the 1820s the town's population was nearly 20,000 – an incredible figure when you reflect that today it is under 3000. During the War of Independence, Ýdhra's merchants provided many of the ships for the Greek forces, and consequently many of the commanders.

ÝDHRA

WATERSIDE TAVERNA, ÝDHRA

Cafés and restaurants

AGORA (AKA YELADHAKIS)

Panayioti Irioti 28, behind the fish market, Égina ☎ 229 70 27 308. Lunch & dinner daily.
The best of three rival seafood ouzerís here (though the others are very good too). Not the most attractive location, but serves wonderful, inexpensive, authentic Greek food (great octopus, sardines, shrimp and other fishy *mezédhes*): accordingly it's usually mobbed and you may have to wait for a table.

ANDONIS

Pérdhika, 9km from Égina Town, Égina ☎ 229 70 61 443. Lunch & dinner daily.
The most popular of the fish tavernas on the harbour here. A little pricey, but the high-quality dishes are still good value.

ANTICA GELATERIA DI ROMA

Farmakopoúlon 3 & Komnímou, just north of Platía Syndágmatos, Náfplio.
Wonderful ice cream made on the premises from fresh fruit and local cream, in a delightfully old-fashioned setting. Also coffee and drinks.

BYZANTIO

Vassiléos Aléxandrou 15, Náfplio Ⓦ www .taverna-byzantio.gr. Dinner daily except Tuesday; also lunch at weekends.
Excellent, friendly taverna on a beautiful street, with a varied menu and large portions. Live Greek music most Friday and Saturday nights.

EPIKOUROS

Pavlou & Fredirikis 33, Dhelfí ☎ 226 50 83 250. Lunch & dinner daily.
One of the best restaurants in Delphi, the wild-boar stew is particularly good – and the view from the terrace is stunning.

FLISVOS

Égina waterfront, by town beach, Égina ☎ 229 70 26 459. Lunch & dinner daily.
Towards the end of a line of similar establishments, an excellent spot for grilled fresh fish and a few meat dishes, at fair prices.

GITONIKO (MANOLIS & CHRISTINA'S)

Ídhra ☎ 229 80 53 615. Lunch & dinner daily.
Hidden away inland, near Áyios Konstandínos church; take the street past the cinema. Very friendly taverna with excellent, well-priced *mayireftá*

at lunch – which runs out early – plus grills (including succulent fish) in the evening. There's a roof terrace too.

ILIOVASILEMA (SUNSET)

Behind the cannons, west side of harbour, Ídhra ☎ 229 80 52 067. Lunch & dinner daily.

An incomparable setting for an end-of-holiday treat or romantic tryst; modern Greek and Italian cuisine that will set you back about €35 per person including wine.

KAKANARAKIS 1986

Vasilíssis Ólgas 18, Náfplio ☎ 275 20 25 371. Dinner only.

Traditional taverna that's been given a style-conscious makeover; still with dependably good *mezédhes* and traditional Greek dishes, plus some Italian-influenced additions and an extensive wine list.

KYRIAKOS

In the alley running behind the fish market, from Platía Iroön to Platía Dhimarhíou, Póros. Lunchtime only, Mon–Sat.

Old-fashioned *mayireftá* establishment popular with locals. Take a look at the kitchen to see what's been prepared that day – when it's all gone, they close.

LEONIDAS

Epidaurus village ☎ 275 20 22 115. Lunch & dinner daily.

A friendly spot with a garden out back; book ahead if your visit coincides with a performance at the ancient theatre. Actors eat here after shows – photos on the wall testify to the patronage of Melina Mercouri, François Mitterrand and Sir Peter Hall.

MYKINAIKO

Mykínes, Mycenae ☎ 275 10 76 724. Lunch & dinner daily.

One of the best in the village in terms of both quality and value, with excellent oven-cooked dishes and a robust, draft red wine known as "Blood of Hercules" to wash it down.

PANAYIOTA

Aráhova ☎ 226 70 32 735. Lunch & dinner daily.

A friendly, family-style taverna high above Aráhova, with fine, good-value lamb dishes, home-baked bread and rich chicken soup.

PARNASSOS

Metókhi, Angístri ☎ 229 70 91 339. Lunch & dinner daily.

It's worth the stiff walk up the hill for the views and the good food here. Dine on *mayireftá* and enjoy the lovely view down to Skála and out towards Égina.

PIRATE

Harbourfront, Ídhra.

Café by day and an increasingly lively bar as the evening wears on, with a young crowd and western music. Among the best prices on the waterfront for coffee, breakfast and sandwiches.

PLATANOS

By the church of Ayíou Yeoryíou, Póros ☎ 229 80 24 249. Dinner only.

One of several evening-only tavernas around the main square of the upper town, serving inexpensive, earthy rural food (the owners also have a butcher's shop) on a vine-covered terrace, washed down with powerful retsina.

VAKHOS

Apóllonos 31, Dhelfí ☎ 226 50 83 250. Lunch & dinner daily.

The view from this family place is stunning, and the food is good-quality traditional fare that's reasonable value for your euros.

ACCOMMODATION

Hotels

Hotels and hostels can be packed to the gills in summer but for most of the year you'll have no problem finding a bed. Having said that, many of the more popular hotels are busy all year round, so it makes sense to book in advance.

Wherever you stay, rooms tend to be small, and noise can be a problem. Pláka, Monastiráki, Makriyiánni and Sýndagma are all atmospheric neighbourhoods within easy walking distance of the main sites; hotels here are also relatively expensive, however, and may be noisy. Somewhat gritty and sleazy but rapidly being gentrified, the bazaar area is the city at its most colourful; most of the larger, modern, business-style hotels are on the busy avenues around Omónia. Koukáki, slightly further out beyond Makriyiánni, has some good, quieter budget options, as do Thissío and Exárhia near the archeological museum. These areas also benefit from good-value local restaurants and the proximity of cinemas, clubs and bars.

Acropolis and Makriyiánni

ACROPOLIS VIEW > Webster 10 Ⓜ Akrópoli Ⓣ 210 92 17 303, Ⓦ www .acropolisview.gr. MAP P.28, POCKET MAP B14 The location is the main attraction here, in what looks like a 1970s apartment block: rooms are small and a bit tired, though a/c and marble bathrooms are pluses. The roof garden has an amazing view of the Acropolis, as do some rooms. Breakfast included. **€90**

ATHENS GATE > Syngroú 10 Ⓜ Akrópoli Ⓣ 210 92 38 302, Ⓦ www.athensgate.gr. MAP P.28,

Hotel prices

Prices for accommodation vary hugely according to the season. The prices quoted here represent the hotel's **cheapest double room in high season**; for much of the year, you'll find rates are significantly lower than this. By law, every room has to display its official rates on the back of the door: it is illegal for a hotelier to charge more than this, and you can normally expect to pay less. Most places have triple and even four-bed rooms, which can be a significant saving for a family or group; more upmarket places may also have family rooms or suites (with two rooms sharing a bathroom).

Breakfast is included in the price at the more expensive hotels and is almost always available at extra cost if it's not included; check what you'll get, however, as the standard Greek hotel breakfast of a cup of weak coffee accompanied by dry cake and jam is rarely worth paying for.

POCKET MAP D14 Very popular four-star, classy, well-run and newly refurbished, but in an exceptionally noisy spot on a major avenue. It's probably best to forego the advertised views of the Temple of Zeus and take a quieter (and cheaper) room at the back; the best views are from the roof terrace anyway. €135

ATHENS STUDIOS > Veïkóu 3a
Ⓜ Akrópoli ☎ 210 92 24 044, Ⓦ www
.athensstudios.gr. MAP P.28, POCKET
MAP D8 Furnished apartments for up to six people, with kitchen, sitting room, TV, a/c and linen provided. Managed by the people who run *Athens Backpackers* (see p.149), and includes use of their bar and facilities. Great value for groups. Apartments from €90

HERODION > Robérto Gálli 4
Ⓜ Akrópoli ☎ 210 92 36 832, Ⓦ www
.herodion.gr. MAP P.28, POCKET MAP
C14 This lovely four-star hotel – albeit not quite as luxurious as the exterior and lobby might lead you to believe – enjoys an enviable position right behind the Acropolis. The roof terrace looks almost straight down to the south slope of the Acropolis. €250

PHILIPPOS > Mitséon 3, Makryiánni
Ⓜ Akrópoli ☎ 210 922 36111, Ⓦ www
.philipposhotel.gr. MAP P.28, POCKET
MAP D8 Three-star sister hotel to the Herodion (see above), the *Philippos* was completely renovated for the 2004 Olympics, though the interior is much less dramatic than the new facade. Very comfortable, well-appointed rooms with TV and a/c. €175

Pláka

ACROPOLIS HOUSE > Kódhrou 6
Ⓜ Sýndagma ☎ 210 32 22 344,
Ⓦ www.acropolishouse.gr. MAP
P.42–43, POCKET MAP D13 A rambling, slightly dilapidated 150-year-old mansion much loved by its regulars – mostly students and academics. Furnishings are individual and some rooms have baths across the hall; not all are a/c, though most are cool. Rates include breakfast and use of fridge. Discounts are offered for longer stays. €70

ADONIS > Kódhrou 3 Ⓜ Sýndagma
☎ 210 32 49 737, Ⓦ www.hotel-adonis
.gr. MAP P.42–43, POCKET MAP D13
A 1960s low-rise pension across the street from *Acropolis House*, with some suites. Rather old-fashioned, but none the worse for it – rooms are comfortable with a/c and TV. The rooftop café has a stunning view of the Acropolis and central Athens. Breakfast included. €80

ATHOS > Patröou 3 Ⓜ Sýndagma
☎ 210 32 21 977, Ⓦ athoshotel.gr.
MAP P.42–43, POCKET MAP D12 This small hotel has cosy, carpeted en-suite rooms (some a little cramped) with TV, a/c and internet. There's also a rooftop bar with Acropolis views. Breakfast included. €100

AVA APARTMENTS & SUITES >
Lysikrátous 9–11 Ⓜ Akrópoli
☎ 210 32 59 000, Ⓦ www.avahotel.gr.
MAP P.42–43, POCKET MAP D14 Between the Temple of Zeus and the Acropolis, *Ava* offers luxurious two-room suites and apartments accommodating up to five people and is ideal for families. All have balconies – some very large – with sideways Acropolis views, as well as small kitchens. Popularity means prices stay high, though. €175

BYRON > Výronos 19 Ⓜ Akrópoli
☎ 210 32 30 327, Ⓦ www.hotel-byron
.gr. MAP P.42–43, POCKET MAP D14
Excellent location within walking distance of the Acropolis and Pláka museums. All rooms are simply furnished, with a/c, TV and free wi-fi, while a few on the upper floors offer balconies and impressive Acropolis views. €120

CENTRAL > Apóllonos 21
Ⓜ Sýndagma ☎ 210 32 34 357,
Ⓦ www.centralhotel.gr. MAP P.42–43,
POCKET MAP D12 This modern three-star hotel has a designer feel, with seagrass or wooden floors, marble bathrooms and excellent soundproofing. It's extremely comfortable and well located, if a bit businessy in style. Family and interconnecting rooms are also available, all with a/c, TV, fridge and internet. There's a large roof terrace with Acropolis views, and a hot tub too. Breakfast included. €120

ELECTRA PALACE > Nikodhímou 18
Ⓜ Sýndagma ☎ 210 33 70 000,
Ⓦ www.electrahotels.gr. MAP P.42–43,
POCKET MAP D13 Right in the heart of
Pláka, this luxurious hotel has excellent
facilities, including indoor and rooftop
pools, plus a gym and sauna. Stunning
if you have an upper-floor suite, whose
balconies have great Acropolis views, but
standard rooms are rather dull. **€200**

HERMES > Apóllonos 19 Ⓜ Sýndagma
☎ 210 32 35 514, Ⓦ www.hermeshotel
.gr. MAP P.42–43, POCKET MAP D12
Friendly and welcoming three-star with
marble bathrooms, polished wood floors
and designer touches in every room,
plus TV, a/c and fridge. Some rooms are
rather small; others have big balconies.
Interconnecting rooms also available.
Breakfast included. **€130**

KOUROS > Kódhrou 11 Ⓜ Sýndagma
☎ 210 32 27 431. MAP P.42–43, POCKET
MAP D13 Faded but atmospheric pension,
with fairly basic facilities: shared baths
and sinks in rooms. The singles are good
value, though, and some rooms have
balconies overlooking the pedestrianized
street. **€45**

PHAEDRA > Herefóndos 16, corner
Adhrianoú Ⓜ Akrópoli ☎ 210 32 38
461, Ⓦ www.hotelphaedra.com. MAP
P.42–43, POCKET MAP D13 Small, simple
rooms with tiled floors, free wi-fi, TV
and a/c, not all en suite (but you get a
private bathroom). The polite, welcoming
management looks after the place well
and it's quiet at night, thanks to a location
at the junction of two pedestrian alleys.
One of the best deals in Pláka. **€65**

STUDENT & TRAVELLER'S INN >
Kydhathinéon 16 Ⓜ Akrópoli
☎ 210 32 44 808, Ⓦ www.student
travellersinn.com. MAP P.42–43, POCKET
MAP D13 A mixture of hotel and hostel,
this is a very friendly, perennially popular
travellers' meeting place. Private quads,
triples and doubles, en-suite or with
shared bath, are clean though not always
quiet. Dorm prices depend on room
size and facilities. The small courtyard
breakfast area/bar, free wi-fi, luggage
storage and travel agency are further
pluses. Dorms **€20–27**, doubles **€70**

Monastiráki and Psyrrí

ATTALOS > Athinás 29 Ⓜ Monastiráki
☎ 210 32 12 801, Ⓦ www.attalos.gr.
MAP P.54–55, POCKET MAP C11 Modern
from the outside but traditional within,
the *Attalos* has bright, comfortable
rooms, well insulated from the noisy
street, all with a/c and TV; there's free
wi-fi in the lobby. Some balcony rooms
on the upper floors have great views
– there's also a roof-terrace bar in the
evenings – but rooms facing the internal
courtyard at the back are generally larger
and quieter. **€90**

CECIL > Athinás 39 Ⓜ Monastiráki
☎ 210 32 17 079, Ⓦ www.cecil.gr.
MAP P.54–55, POCKET MAP C11 This
formerly run-down, 150-year-old
pension has been lovingly restored. The
attractively decorated, good-sized rooms
(some internal) have polished wooden
floors, a/c and TV, and there's a lovely
wrought-iron lift and a roof garden.
Helpful management too. Breakfast
included. **€95**

METROPOLIS > Mitropóleos 46
Ⓜ Sýndagma/Monastiráki ☎ 210 32
17 469, Ⓦ www.hotelmetropolis.gr.
MAP P.54–55, POCKET MAP D12 Right
by the cathedral, the friendly *Metropolis*
has simple, plainly furnished rooms
with vinyl floors, each with a good-sized
balcony, a/c and TV, plus Acropolis views
from the upper floors; some have shared
bathrooms. **€65**

OCHRE AND BROWN > Leokoríou 7
Ⓜ Thissío ☎ 210 33 12 950, Ⓦ www
.oandbhotel.com. MAP P.54–55, POCKET
MAP B11 Understated boutique hotel with
just 11 rooms, one of which is a large
suite with private terrace and views; all
rooms have free wi-fi and satellite TV, as
well as DVD and CD players. Friendly as
well as luxurious and elegant, plus a great
location on the fringes of Psyrrí. **€150**

PLAKA > Kapnikaréas 7, corner
Mitropóleos Ⓜ Sýndagma/Monastiráki
☎ 210 32 22 096, Ⓦ www.plakahotel
.gr. MAP P.54–55, POCKET MAP C12
Excellent location, friendly management
and quiet refurbished rooms with TV,
a/c and fridge make this a good choice,

though popularity means it's often full. The roof garden has particularly good Acropolis views. Breakfast included. €130

Thissío, Gázi and Áno Petrálona

ERIDANUS > Pireós 78 Ⓜ Thissío ☎ 210 52 05 360, Ⓦ www.eridanus.gr. MAP P.65, POCKET MAP A10 A boutique hotel with luxurious facilities, including green-marble bathrooms with massage showers, plus there are great Acropolis views from the roof terrace and some rooms. It's mainly business-oriented, but deals are sometimes available. €195

PHIDIAS > Apostólou Pávlou 39 Ⓜ Thissío ☎ 210 34 59 511, Ⓦ www .phidias.gr. MAP P.65, POCKET MAP A12 With an enviable position in Thissío overlooking the Acropolis, at the heart of a newly fashionable area crammed with designer cafés, the Phidias has cosy if rather dated rooms, with TV and a/c. It's probably overdue for a makeover, but in the meantime is decent value, especially the rooms at the front, which have balconies and fabulous views. Breakfast included. €80

Sýndagma and around

ARETHUSA > Mitropóleos 6–8 and Níkis 12 Ⓜ Sýndagma ☎ 210 32 29 431, Ⓦ www.arethusahotel.gr. MAP P.75, POCKET MAP E12 Staff at this low-key high-rise are friendly, and though the rooms are a little tired, they're well soundproofed, with a/c and TV, and are good value considering the excellent location. €80

GRANDE BRETAGNE > Vasiléos Yioryíou 1, Platía Sýndagma Ⓜ Sýndagma ☎ 210 33 30 000, Ⓦ www.grandebretagne.gr. MAP P.75, POCKET MAP E12 If someone else is paying, try to get them to put you up at the Grande Bretagne, the grandest of all Athens' hotels, with the finest location in town. Recently refurbished, it really is magnificent, with every conceivable facility, though treatments in the spa cost more than a night at many hotels. €300

Platía Omonías and the bazaar

THE ALASSIA > Sokrátous 50, Omónia Ⓜ Omónia ☎ 210 52 74 000, Ⓦ www.thealassia.com.gr. MAP P.82, POCKET MAP D3 Decorated in minimalist style with lots of dark-wood veneers. Rooms are small but well soundproofed (you're just off Platía Omonías here) and with every comfort, including designer bathrooms. €80

ART HOTEL > Márni 27 Ⓜ Omónia ☎ 210 52 40 501, Ⓦ www.arthotel athens.gr. MAP P.82, POCKET MAP D3 Not the greatest location, and on a rather noisy, scruffy street, but nevertheless a very pleasant boutique hotel in a refurbished 1920s building with individually designed rooms. Thoughtful touches include Korres toiletries in the marble bathrooms, and there's a substantial buffet breakfast. €80

ATHENS CENTER SQUARE > Arostogítonos 15 Ⓜ Monastiráki ☎ 210 32 11 770, Ⓦ www.athens centersquarehotel.gr. MAP P.82, POCKET MAP C10 This new, budget boutique hotel, directly above the fruit and vegetable market, is handy for Psyrrí too, though the area can be rather insalubrious at night. Smallish but very well-appointed rooms with a/c, flat-screen TVs and free wi-fi, some with balconies. Very good online deals often available. Breakfast included. €120

DELPHI ART HOTEL > Ayíou Konstandínou 27 Ⓜ Omónia ☎ 210 52 44 004, Ⓦ www.delphiart hotel.com. MAP P.82, POCKET MAP D4 Right by the National Theatre and Áyios Konstantínos church, this 1930s mansion has been lavishly restored with Art Nouveau touches and eclectic, individual furnishings. Facilities include wi-fi throughout (for a charge), and jacuzzi baths in some rooms. Breakfast included. €80

EVROPI > Satovriándhou 7
Ⓜ Omónia ☎ 210 52 23 081. MAP P.82, POCKET MAP D3 Extremely basic but great-value old-fashioned hotel with spacious rooms occupied only by bed, bedside table and ceiling fan, along with a concrete enclosure for en-suite shower. Reasonably quiet, despite being only a block from Platía Omonías; inexpensive single rooms available. **€50**

FRESH HOTEL > Sofokléous 26
Ⓜ Omónia ☎ 210 52 48 511, Ⓦ www.freshhotel.gr. MAP P.82, POCKET MAP C10 Glossy, high-end hotel in the heart of the market area. Lavish use of colour, elegant furnishings and great lighting and bathrooms, though you do wonder how long it will stay looking fresh; some rooms are tiny, and the area can be a bit seedy after dark. Facilities include wi-fi throughout and an elegant rooftop pool, bar and restaurant, popular with non-residents. **€150**

TEMPI > Eólou 29 Ⓜ Monastiráki
☎ 210 32 13 175, Ⓦ www.tempihotel .gr. MAP P.82, POCKET MAP C11 A long-time favourite with budget travellers: book exchange, free wi-fi, drinks and shared kitchen, plus handy affiliated travel agency. Rooms are simple and tiny and half have shared facilities, but all are a/c and the view of the flower market at Ayía Iríni across the quiet pedestrian walkway is enchanting. Within walking distance of most central sights. **€57**

The Archeological Museum, Exárhia and Neápoli

CENTROTEL > Peoníou 11a
Ⓜ Larissa ☎ 210 82 58 010, Ⓦ www.centrotel.gr. MAP P.90–91, POCKET MAP D1 A smart, clean, modern and extremely well-run hotel. Many of the well-appointed rooms have balconies and jacuzzi baths. The main drawbacks are that it is on a nondescript street in a nondescript neighbourhood, and the fact

that popularity means prices are rarely discounted. Free wi-fi. Breakfast not included. **€80**

EXARCHION > Themistokléous 55, Platía Exárhia Ⓜ Omónia
☎ 210 38 01 256, Ⓦ www.exarchion .com. MAP P.90–91, POCKET MAP E3 This big, 1960s high-rise is a great deal less fancy inside than you might imagine, despite its recent refurbishment. Still, it's good value if you want to be at the heart of Exárhia's nightlife, there's free wi-fi, and the simple rooms have TV, a/c and fridge. The upper floors are quieter, with better views. **€65**

MUSEUM > Bouboulínas 16
Ⓜ Viktorías/Omónia ☎ 210 38 05 611, Ⓦ www.museumhotel.gr. MAP P.90–91, POCKET MAP E3 Very pleasant, international-style hotel (part of the Best Western chain) right behind the National Archeological Museum and the Polytekhnío. Rooms in the new wing, which has triples, quads and small suites ideal for families, are better but slightly more expensive. **€90**

ORION AND DRYADES >
Anexartisías 5 Ⓜ Omónia
☎ 210 36 27 362, Ⓦ www.orion -dryades.com. MAP P.90–91, POCKET MAP F3 Quiet, well-run twin hotels across from the Lófos Stréfi park – a steep uphill walk from almost anywhere. Reception is in the cheaper Orion, which has shared bathrooms, a kitchen, and a communal area on the roof with an amazing view of central Athens. All rooms in the Dryades are en suite with a/c and TV; there's wi-fi throughout, for a charge. **€45–75**

Kolonáki and Lykavitós Hill

PERISCOPE > Háritos 22, Kolonáki
Ⓜ Evangelismós ☎ 210 72 97 200, Ⓦ www.yeshotels.gr. MAP P.100–101, POCKET MAP G5 Designer minimalism on a shopping street in Kolonáki; the name refers to a periscope camera set up on the roof, which guests can control and view the pictures. The

luxurious rooms tend to be small (though the penthouse suite has its own rooftop hot tub) and the quiet setting can be compromised by the fact that the bar downstairs is a popular late-night hangout. Excellent breakfast included. **€135**

ST GEORGE LYCABETTUS >
Kleoménous 75, Kolonáki
Ⓜ Evangelismós ☎ 210 72 90 711, Ⓦ www.sglycabettus.gr. MAP P.100–101, POCKET MAP G5 A luxury boutique hotel and an Athenian classic, with a position high on Lykavitós Hill in ritzy Kolonáki overlooking the city. Abundant marble and leather in the public areas, plus a very pleasant rooftop pool, and bars and a restaurant popular with wealthy young Athenians. Some of the rooms are rather small, however, and there's no point staying here if you don't pay extra for the view. Courtyard view **€150**, Acropolis view **€180**

Koukáki, Pangráti and Mets

ART GALLERY >
Erekthíou 5, Koukáki
Ⓜ Syngroú-Fix ☎ 210 92 38 376, Ⓦ www.artgalleryhotel.gr. MAP P.114, POCKET MAP D8 This slightly old-fashioned, family-owned pension with many repeat customers is named for its abundance of original artworks. Helpful staff, a convenient location a short walk from the metro, plus a bountiful breakfast (at extra cost) served on a terrace with Acropolis view. **€90**

MARBLE HOUSE >
Cul-de-sac off A. Zínni 35a, Koukáki Ⓜ Syngroú-Fix ☎ 210 92 34 058, Ⓦ www.marble house.gr. MAP P.114, POCKET MAP C9 The best value in Koukáki, family run and friendly. Simple rooms with and without private bath, with fans and a/c (for extra charge). It's often full, so call ahead. **€45**

Hostels

HOSTEL APHRODITE >
Inárdhou 12, between Alakmenous and Mikhaïl Vódha Ⓜ Viktorías ☎ 210 88 39 249, Ⓦ www.hostelaphrodite.com. MAP P.90–91, POCKET MAP D1 Friendly, clean, IYHA-recognized hostel with some private en-suite doubles and triples, in a quiet residential neighbourhood. A/c available at extra charge; other facilities include breakfast room/bar, luggage storage and free internet. Discounts for YHA cardholders. Dorms **€17–25**, doubles **€50**

ATHENS BACKPACKERS >
Mákri 12, Makriyiánni Ⓜ Akrópoli ☎ 210 92 24 044, Ⓦ www.backpackers.gr. MAP P.28, POCKET MAP D14 Very central Athenian-Australian-run hostel with few frills, but clean rooms, communal kitchen, internet access, bar, fabulous rooftop view and great atmosphere. Dorms **€22–28**

ATHENS INTERNATIONAL YOUTH HOSTEL >
Víktoros Ougó 16 Ⓜ Metaxouryío ☎ 210 52 32 540, Ⓦ www.athens-international.com. MAP P.82, POCKET MAP C3 The old official youth hostel is a huge affair, with 140 beds over 7 floors in 2- and 4-bed rooms. Recently given a coat of paint, but still basic, it is always busy so it's best to book in advance; discounts for YHA cardholders. Dorms **€17**, doubles **€55**

PAGRATION YOUTH HOSTEL >
Dhamáreos 75, Pangráti, buses #2 and #11 from Omónia via Sýndagma; #203 or #204 (or 15–20min walk) from Ⓜ Evangelismós ☎ 210 75 19 530, Ⓦ www.athens-yhostel.com. MAP P.112, POCKET MAP H8 A bit out of the way but friendly and good value, in a decent, quiet neighbourhood with plenty of local restaurants and lively nightlife. The dorms are basic and sleep 5–6. There's free use of the kitchen and communal area with TV, though you pay extra for the washing machine and hot water. There's no sign on the door, so look for the green gate. Dorms **€15**

STUDENT AND TRAVELLER'S INN
> See p.146.

Arrival

A new airport and substantial investment in transport links have transformed Athens. The airport is linked to the city by bus, metro and a fast expressway, while the metro, plenty of taxis and city buses service Pireás for those arriving by boat. Even driving in is relatively straightforward thanks to new roads – though parking or getting around the centre by car is only for the brave.

By air

Athens' Elefthéríos Venizélos airport (☎ 210 35 30 000, ⊛ www.aia.gr) is at Spáta, 33km southeast of the city. It's a slick operation, with excellent access to Athens and to major roads bypassing the city. Facilities include ATMs and banks with money-changing facilities on all levels, plus luggage storage with Pacific (☎ 210 35 30 160, ⊛ www.pacifictravel.gr) on the Arrivals level. There's also the usual array of travel agencies and car rental places, plus a very handy official EOT tourist office (Mon–Sat 9am–7pm, Sun 10am–4pm; ☎ 210 35 30 445) on the Arrivals level. Finally, there's a one-room museum displaying artefacts discovered in the area – mainly during construction of the airport – which is much more interesting than you might expect.

Public transportation from the airport is excellent. The metro and suburban trains share a station. The **metro** (€6 one way, €10 return, discounts for multiple tickets, or €15 for a 3-day pass including all public transport) is usually more convenient, taking you straight into the heart of the city where you can change to the other metro lines at either Monastiráki or Sýndagma. Trains run every thirty minutes from 6.30am to 11.30pm, and take around forty minutes. The **suburban train** (same fares) offers direct trains to the northern suburbs and Corinth but for Laríssis station in the centre and Pireás, you have to change at Neratziotissa.

Buses are slightly slower, especially at rush hours, but they're also much cheaper, run all night and offer direct links to other parts of the city, including Pireás. The most useful are the #X95 to Sýndagma square, via Ethnikí Ámyna metro and the Hilton (at least three an hour, day and night) and #X96 to the port at Pireás via Glyfádha and the beach suburbs (at least two an hour, day and night). Tickets cost €3.20; you can buy them from a booth beside the stops or on the bus – make sure you have small change.

Taxis are subject to the vagaries of traffic and can take anything from forty minutes (at night) to an hour and forty minutes (at rush hour) to reach the centre; the daytime fare should be roughly €32 to central Athens or Pireás, including luggage and tolls.

By ferry

The simplest way to get to Athens from Pireás is by metro (5am to after midnight) For the airport, take express bus #X96 (every 20min 7am–9pm, every 40min 9pm–7am). Taxis between Pireás and central Athens should cost around €10, including luggage; getting a taxi when a ferry arrives is no easy matter, though – you'll need to be pushy, and almost certainly have to share.

Getting around

Athens is served by slow but ubiquitous buses, a fast, mostly modern metro system, and a tram service that runs from the centre to the beach suburbs. Taxis are also plentiful and, for short journeys in town, exceptionally cheap. Most public transportation operates from around 5am to just after midnight, though the metro continues till 2.30am on Friday and Saturday nights and a few buses – including those to the airport – run all night. Driving is a traffic-crazed nightmare, and parking far worse. If you do have a car, you're strongly advised to find somewhere to park it for the duration of your stay.

The metro

The expanded **metro** system (ⓦ www.amel.gr) is much the easiest way to get around central Athens; it's fast, quiet and user-friendly. It consists of three lines: **Line 1** (green; Pireás to Kifissiá) is the original section, with useful stops in the centre at Thissío,

Monastiráki, Omónia and Viktorías; **Line 2** (red; Áyios Antónios to Áyios Dhimítrios) has central stops at Omónia, Sýndagma and Akrópoli; and **Line 3** (blue; Egaléo to the airport) passes through Monastiráki and Sýndagma. Some of the new stations are attractions in their own right, displaying artefacts unearthed in their excavation (numerous important discoveries were made) and other items of local interest – Sýndagma and Akrópoli are particularly interesting central ones.

When travelling on the metro you need to know the final stop in the direction you're heading, as that is how the platforms are identified ("To Pireás" for example); there are plenty of maps in the stations.

Buses

Athens' **bus** network (ⓦ www.oasa.gr) is extensive and cheap, but pretty confusing and very crowded at peak times. Routes, where relevant, are detailed in the text. The most straightforward are the **trolley-buses**: #1 connects Laríssis train station with Omónia, Sýndagma and

Tickets and passes

The easiest and least stressful way to travel is with a pass. A **three-day ticket** including transport to and from the airport and the #400 tourist sightseeing bus costs €15, available only at the airport and at Sýndagma, Omónia and Pireás metro stations. Otherwise a **one-day imerísio** costs €3 and can be used on buses, trolleybuses, trams and the metro in central Athens. You validate it once, at the beginning of your first journey, and it is good for 24 hours from then. A 24-hour pass including tourist bus #400 is available for €5 (see box, p.154). A **weekly pass** costs €10; again it must be validated on first use. For **single journeys**, a €1 ticket is valid on all city-centre transport for ninety minutes from validation.

Tickets and passes can be bought from machines and ticket offices in any metro station, from machines on tram platforms, and from booths near major bus stops – you can buy several at once and then validate them as necessary. All tickets must be validated (once only) before you start your journey, in the machines at the top of the metro stairs, on the tram platform or carriage, or as you board a bus.

Koukáki; #2, #4, #5, #9, #11 and #15 all link Sýndagma with Omónia and the National Archeological Museum on 28 Oktovríou (Patissíon). There are also scores of regular **city buses**, serving countless routes out into the straggling suburbs and beyond; at most of the major stops there are helpful information booths.

The tram

The modern **tram** network (ⓦ www .tramsa.gr) is a great way to get to the coastal suburbs and the beach. The tram runs from Leofóros Amalías, just off Sýndagma, to the coast, where it branches. To the right it heads northwest towards Pireás, terminating at SEF (the Stádhio Eirínis ké Fílias or Peace and Friendship Stadium), an interchange with Metro line 1 at Néo Fáliro, and within walking distance of Pireás's leisure harbours. Left, the tram lines run southwest along the coast to Glyfádha. The tram doesn't automatically stop at every station, so push the bell if you're on board, or wave it down if you're on the platform.

Taxis

Athenian **taxis** can seem astonishingly cheap – trips around the city centre will rarely run above €5, which means for a group of three or four they cost little more than the metro. Longer trips are also reasonable value: the airport only costing around €30 and Pireás €8–10 from the centre – the exact amount determined by traffic and amount of luggage. All officially licensed cars are yellow and have a red-on-white number plate. You can wave them down on the street, pick them up at ranks in most of the major travel termini and central squares, or get your hotel to call for one.

Make sure the meter is switched on when you get in. If it's "not working", find another taxi. One legitimate way that taxi drivers increase their income is to pick up other passengers along the way. There is no fare-sharing: each passenger (or group of passengers) pays the full fare for their journey. So if you're picked up by an already-occupied taxi, memorize the meter reading; you'll pay from that point on, plus the €0.85 initial tariff. When hailing an occupied taxi, call out your destination, so the driver can decide whether you suit him or not.

Tours

Most travel agencies offer a variety of **tours** out of Athens, as well as day- or half-day tours of the city. The latter normally include a bus drive around the highlights and a guided tour of the Acropolis and its museum for around €35. You could also take the **Sunshine Express** "Happy Train" ride, which sets out from the Platía Paliás Agorás (on Eólou, just off Adhrianoú; ⓦ www.sunshine-express.gr) and clatters past most of the major sites for an hour or so (€5, children €3), or the similar service that runs from Sýndagma at the top of Ermoú. Alternatively, the **#400 city bus** offers a hop-on, hop-off service passing most major sites. Tickets (€5, purchased on the bus) are valid for 24 hours on all public transport. Major stops are at the Archeological Museum, Sýndagma and Omónia.

Directory A–Z

Cinema

Athens is a great place to catch a movie. In summer, **outdoor screens** spring up in every neighbourhood of the city for a quintessentially Greek film-going experience. Tickets are around €7–8 for outdoor screenings, €9–12 for first-run fare at a midtown theatre. Films are almost always shown in the original language with Greek subtitles (a good way to increase your vocabulary, though remember that the original language may not be English). Downtown **indoor cinemas** are concentrated on the three main thoroughfares connecting Omónia and Sýndagma; and in Ambelókipi, around the junctions of Leofóros Alexándhras and Kifissías. Central and reliable outdoor venues include rooftop Cine Pari, Kydhathinéon 22, Pláka (☎ 210 32 22 071); Thission, Apostólou Pávlou 7 in Thissío (☎ 210 34 70 980); Psyrri, Sarrí 40–44, Psyrrí (☎ 210 32 12 476); Zefyros, Tróon 36 in Áno Petrálona (☎ 210 34 62 677); and Vox, Themistokléous 82, Platía Exarhíon in Exárhia (☎ 210 33 01 020).

Crime

Athens is among the safest cities in Europe, though inevitably crime rates are rising and the economic crisis is unlikely to help; the area around Omónia and the market can feel particularly intimidating at night. The most common crime to affect tourists is bag-snatching, especially from a passing moped. If you are a victim of crime it's best to first contact the multilingual **Tourist Police** (☎ 171), who can guide you through the system if necessary.

Electricity

Voltage is 220V a/c, with standard European round two-pin plugs.

Embassies and consulates

Most major **embassies** are in Kolonáki or Ambelókipi, on or not far from Leofóros Vassilísis Sofías. They include: **Australia**, Level 6, Thon Building, cnr Kifissiás & Alexandhrás, Ambelókipi 7 ☎ 210 87 04 000, ⓦwww.ausemb.gr (Ⓜ Ambelókipi); **Canada**, Ioánnou Yennadhíou 4 ☎ 210 72 73 400, ⓦwww.athens.gc.ca (Ⓜ Evangelismós); **Ireland**, Vassiléos Konstandínou 7 ☎ 210 72 32 771, in Pangráti near the Panathenaic Stadium; **New Zealand** (honorary consulate), Kifissiás 76, Ambelókipi ☎ 210 69 24 136 (Ⓜ Ambelókipi); **South Africa**, Kifissiás 60, Maroúsi ☎ 210 610 6645 (Ⓜ Panormóu); **UK**, Ploutárhou 1, Kolonáki ☎ 210 72 72 600, ⓦ ukingreece.fco.gov.uk (Ⓜ Evangelismós); **US**, Vassilísis Sofías 91 ☎ 210 72 12 951, ⓦathens .usembassy.gov (Ⓜ Mégaro Mousikís).

Ferries

Almost any travel agent in Athens can sell you **ferry tickets**, but they don't necessarily represent all companies, so shop around to be sure you're not taking a roundabout route. In Pireás, there's far more choice. Unless you want a cabin, there's rarely any need to book ahead.

Emergency numbers

European emergency number ☎ 112; Ambulance ☎ 166; Fire ☎ 199; Police ☎ 100; Tourist police ☎ 171.

Health

English-speaking SOS **doctors** are on ☎ 1016, and will come to you in your hotel room – at a price. The largest central **hospital** is Evangelismós at Ipsilándhou 45, Kolonáki (☎ 210 72 01 000; Ⓜ Evangelismós). You'll find a list of hospitals, and a few adverts for English-speaking doctors, in the weekly *Athens News*; ⓦ athens.us embassy.gov has hospital addresses and a list of practitioners (under Special Consular Services). Most doctors speak at least some English, and medical care is generally very good, though nursing and after-care tend to rely on the help of family.

There are a number of large **pharmacies** (*farmakía*) around Omónia, especially on 28 Oktovríou and Panepistimíou; many also sell homeopathic remedies. Standard hours are Mon & Wed 8am–2.30pm, Tues, Thurs & Fri 8am–2pm & 5.30–8.30pm. For out-of-hours pharmacies, see the weekly *Athens News*;

a list of these is also on display in many pharmacies, or call ☎ 107.

Internet

There are plenty of **internet cafés** throughout the centre, charging €1.50–4/hr. 24-hour places include: Bits & Bytes, Kapnikaréas 19, off Adhrianoú in Pláka, and Café 4U, Ippokrátous 44 in Exárhia. Many hotels have wi-fi and there are also numerous free wireless zones, including Sýndagma square.

Left luggage

Best arranged with your hotel; many places will guard your luggage for free or for a nominal amount while you head off for a few days. Pacific Travel, Níkis 26, Sýndagma and at the airport (☎ 210 32 41 007, ⓦ www .pacifictravel.gr) charges around €9 per item per day.

Money

Standard currency in Greece is the **euro**, divided into 100 leptá (cents).

Public holidays

Virtually all shops and businesses will close for **public holidays**, as will smaller sites and private museums. Plenty of restaurants should stay open, however, and the largest state-run sites and museums (including the Acropolis) are not just open, but free.

Jan 1 New Year's Day

Jan 6 Epiphany

Feb or March: Clean Monday (Kathará Dheftéra; March 7, 2011; February 27, 2012; March 18, 2013). On Clean Monday – the beginning of Lent, 48 days before Easter – the tradition is to fly kites and walk in the country; this is followed by pre-Lenten Carnival celebrations, with street concerts, eating and drinking to excess, and bashing people over the head with plastic hammers.

March 25 Independence Day

April or May Easter (April 24, 2011; April 15, 2012; May 5, 2013). Good Friday and Easter Monday are public holidays. An intensely religious festival, with plenty of feasting afterwards.

May 1 May Day. The city is usually brought to a standstill by huge Leftist demonstrations.

May or June Whit Monday (Áyion Pnévma; June 13, 2011; June 4, 2012; June 24, 2013)

Aug 15 Assumption of the Virgin

Oct 28 Óhi Day

Dec 25 & 26 Christmas

Major **credit cards** are accepted virtually everywhere, though perhaps with reluctance at the cheaper tavernas and bars. **Banks** are open Monday to Thursday 8am to 2.30pm, Friday 8am to 2pm; several banks with longer hours can be found around Sýndagma, plus there are numerous currency-exchange places (generally with worse rates) in Pláka and around Sýndagma. Almost every bank in the centre has an ATM.

Opening hours

Traditionally **shops and offices** open from 8.30/9am until 1.30 or 2.30pm, when there is a long break for the hottest part of the day. Most places, except banks and government offices, then reopen in the late afternoon, from about 5.30 to 8.30pm; they're closed on Sundays, and often on Saturday, Monday and Wednesday afternoons. However, an increasing number of stores, especially in the centre and above all the tourist shops in Pláka, now remain open throughout the day. Hours can also vary between summer and winter (usually Oct–March & April–Sept). For pharmacy opening hours, see "Health"; for banking hours, see "Money"; for post office hours, see "Post".

Phones

Phone-card booths are ubiquitous, and calling cards for cheap overseas calls are sold at many kiosks, especially around Omónia. There's excellent **mobile phone** coverage everywhere, including throughout the metro system.

Post

The main **post office** is on Sýndagma (cnr Mitropóleos; Mon–Fri 7.30am–8pm, Sat 7.30am–2pm, Sun 9am–1.30pm). There are also major branches (Mon–Fri 7.30am–2.30pm) at Mitrópoleos 60 near the cathedral, near Omónia at Eólou 100 (also open Sat), and on Platía Kótzia. Queues can be very long, so be sure you're at the right counter – there are often separate ones (with shorter lines) for stamps and parcels.

Smoking

Greeks smoke heavily, often in crowded public places such as cafés, restaurants and bars, although officially it's banned. Public transport is non-smoking, as are many offices, but in defiance of the law only a small minority of places to eat or drink will have effective non-smoking areas.

Time

Greek time is always two hours ahead of Britain. For North America, the difference is seven hours for Eastern Standard Time, ten hours for Pacific Standard Time, with an extra hour plus or minus for those few weeks when one place is on daylight saving and the other isn't.

Tipping

Large tips are not expected. Restaurant bills include a service element, so here, as well as in taxis, hotels, etc, only small change is expected.

Tourist information

The Greek National Tourist Office has a central **information office** at Amalías 26 (Mon–Fri 9am–7pm; ☎ 210 33 10 392, ⓦ www.gnto.gr). This is a useful first stop for information, and they have a good free map as well as information on opening hours, bus and ferry schedules, and so on. If you are arriving by plane, you can save time by calling in at the airport branch (see p.152).

Listings information in English is limited; a number of free monthly or weekly publications distributed to hotels have a few what's-on listings, but these are not always accurate; better are the weekly *Athens News* (published Friday; Ⓦ www.athensnews.gr), with full cinema listings in English and coverage of most major events, or the daily local edition of the *International Herald Tribune*. More exhaustive listings including music, clubs, restaurants and bars, but in Greek only, can be found in local weekly *Athinorama*, and in various free publications which can be picked up in galleries, record shops and the like.

Travelling with children

With its heat and preponderance of classical sites, Athens may not be the most immediately attractive city for children. But they will be warmly welcomed everywhere, most hotels have family rooms, and there are plenty of outdoor activities, from climbing hills to heading to the beach, to leaven a diet of antiquity.

Travellers with disabilities

Hotels throughout Athens were refurbished in the run-up to the Olympics, and many have accessible rooms and other facilities; there's even a lift to the top of the Acropolis. However, the infrastructure of the city is tricky for people in wheelchairs or with limited mobility. Pavements are rarely smooth and frequently blocked, there are many steep streets, and the ground at most archeological sites is extremely uneven. The new Metro has excellent lifts from pavement level direct to the platforms, but there's often a large gap between the platform and the train.

The Athens and Epidaurus Festival

The annual **Athens and Epidaurus Festival** encompasses a broad spectrum of cultural events: most famously ancient Greek theatre (performed, in modern Greek, at the Herodes Atticus Theatre on the south slope of the Acropolis), but also modern theatre, traditional and contemporary dance, classical music, jazz, traditional Greek music and even a smattering of rock.

The **Herodes Atticus Theatre** (see p.35) is a memorable place to watch a performance on a warm summer's evening – although you should avoid the cheapest seats, unless you bring along a pair of binoculars and a cushion. Other festival venues include the open-air **Lykavitós Theatre** on Lykavitós Hill (see p.99), and the two ancient theatres at **Epidaurus** (see p.134). For the latter, you can buy inclusive trips from Athens from the festival box office, either by coach or boat – the two-hour boat trip includes dinner on board on the way home.

Performances are scheduled from late May right through to early October, although the exact dates vary each year. It's worth booking in advance (credit card bookings on ☎ 210 32 72 000 and at Ⓦ www.greekfestival.gr); tickets go on sale three weeks before the event.

As well as online, programmes are available from tourist offices or from the festival box office in the arcade at Panepistimíou 39 (Mon–Fri 8.30am–4pm, Sat 9am–2pm). There are also box offices at the Herodes Atticus Theatre (daily 9am–2pm and 5–8pm) and at Epidaurus (Mon–Thurs 9am–2pm and 5–8pm, Fri & Sat 9.30am–9.30pm), for events at those venues only.

Chronology

c5000 BC > First Neolithic settlements around the rock of the Acropolis.

c1500 BC > Mycenaean palace-fortress established on the Acropolis – traces of its walls can still be seen.

c1200–600 BC > Following the fall of Mycenae, Athens develops as an independent city-state. Draco's draconian law code is published in 621 BC.

594 BC > Amid growing political unrest, Solon appointed as ruler with a mandate to reduce the power of the city's aristocratic clique. His reforms lay the foundations of democracy.

560 BC > The "tyrant" Peisistratos seizes power; under his populist leadership the wealth, power and influence of Athens grow hugely.

510 BC > Kleisthenes introduces the final elements of Athenian democracy, creating a city-state run by its male citizens.

490 BC > Battle of Marathon. The Athenians and their allies defeat a far larger Persian force.

480 BC > Athens sacked and burned to the ground by the Persians. The same year, the Persians are comprehensively defeated at the naval battle of Salamis, off Athens. Victory brings peace and secures Athens' position as Greece's leading city-state.

480–430 BC > The Golden Age. Under the leadership of Pericles, Athens flourishes in every area. The great buildings on the Acropolis and elsewhere – including the Parthenon – are constructed, and in sculpture, pottery, drama and philosophy the city attains unprecedented heights.

431–404 BC > The Peloponnesian War against perennial enemy Sparta ends in defeat and a long period of gradual decline, though in the following century Athens can still boast the likes of Plato and Aristotle.

338 BC > Philip of Macedon takes control of the city.

146 BC > Roman conquest.

86 BC > Caught up in Rome's domestic wars, Athens is besieged and sacked by Sulla.

52 AD > St Paul preaches to the Athenians from the Areopagus.

117–138 AD > Reign of Emperor Hadrian, the city's last great benefactor of ancient times.

380 > Christianity becomes the official religion of the Roman Empire, now ruled from Byzantium (Constantinople). Athens' temples gradually converted to Christian use; early churches built.

529 > Under Justinian I, the last "pagan" (i.e. Platonic) schools closed, and the final temples converted to Christian use.

1300–1456 > Athens passes through the hands of various European powers: Franks, Catalans, Florentines and Venetians.

1453 > Sultan Mehmet II conquers Constantinople.

1456 > The Ottomans take control of Athens. Under Turkish rule for almost 400 years, Athens is a backwater. The Parthenon and other temples are converted to mosques.

1684 > The Temple of Athena Nike dismantled by the Ottomans in their ongoing wars with the Venetians.

1687 > The roof and much of the structure of the Parthenon destroyed in Venetian bombardment.

1801–1812 > Lord Elgin removes statues and friezes from the Parthenon, sparking continuing controversy over the "Elgin Marbles".

1821 > Greek War of Independence begins.

1828 > First Greek National Assembly held, in Náfplio.

1834 > Capital of Greece moved to Athens by Otto, the new king appointed by the Great Powers. Construction of the modern city begins.

1896 > First modern Olympic Games held in Athens.

1914–18 > World War I sees Greece initially neutral, but civil war breaks out with anti-royalist, pro-allied forces: continues intermittently for the next twenty years.

1923 > Following a disastrous Greek military campaign in Turkey, the Treaty of Lausanne provides for a massive exchange of populations between Greece and Turkey – over a million refugees arrive, many settling in Athens and Pireás.

1941–44 > German occupation; many die of famine in winter of 1941–42.

1944–49 > Greek Civil War.

1950s–60s > Peace and American aid sees rapid economic growth, and huge expansion of Athens in unremittingly ugly development.

1967–74 > Colonels' junta sees army seize power.

1973 > Massacre of students at the Athens Polytechnic marks the beginning of the end for the colonels.

1974 > Democracy restored.

1981 > Greece elects socialist government and joins EU.

1990s > First serious attempts to tackle pollution problems. Increasing growth and stability rewarded with the promise of the 2004 Olympics.

2001 > Euro introduced, amid allegations that the economic statistics have been fixed.

2004 > Despite last-minute preparations and massive cost over-runs, the Olympics are a huge success, with a lasting legacy in terms of infrastructure and transformation of the city's reputation.

2009–10 > Debt crisis and austerity programmes. Greece is forced to go to the EU and IMF to avoid defaulting on its ever-mounting debt. The vicious austerity measures required, above all cutting back on civil service pay and pensions and increasing taxes, lead to widespread domestic unrest and violence.

Greek

You can get by in Athens speaking only English – in the tourist areas certainly there'll always be someone who can speak it fluently. Away from the centre you may struggle occasionally, but even here an English-speaker is rarely far away. However, the effort of mastering a few Greek words is well repaid, and will transform your status from that of dumb tourístas to the more honourable one of xénos/xéni, a word which can mean foreigner, traveller and guest all rolled into one.

Pronunciation

On top of the usual difficulties of learning a new language, Greek presents the additional problem of an entirely separate **alphabet**. Despite initial appearances, this is in practice fairly easily mastered and is a skill that will help enormously if you are going to get around independently. In addition, certain combinations of letters have unexpected results. Remember that the correct **stress** (marked with an accent) is also crucial.

Set out below is the Greek alphabet, the system of transliteration used in this book, and a brief aid to pronunciation.

Greek transliteration

Α, α	a	a as in father
Β, β	v	v as in vet
Γ, γ	y/g	y as in yes except before consonants or a, o or ou when it's a breathy, hard g
Δ, δ	dh	th as in then
Ε, ε	e	e as in get
Ζ, ζ	z	z sound
Η, η	i	i as in ski
Θ, θ	th	th as in theme
Ι, ι	i	i as in ski
Κ, κ	k	k sound
Λ, λ	l	l sound
Μ, μ	m	m sound
Ν, ν	n	n sound
Ξ, ξ	x	x sound
Ο, ο	o	o as in toad
Π, π	p	p sound
Ρ, ρ	r	r sound
Σ, σ, ς	s	s sound, although z before m or g
Τ, τ	t	t sound
Υ, υ	y	y as in barely
Φ, φ	f	f sound
Χ, χ	h/kh	harsh h sound, like ch in loch, before vowels, kh before consonants
Ψ, ψ	ps	ps as in lips
Ω, ω	o	o as in toad, indistinguishable from o

Combinations and diphthongs

AI, αι	e	e as in hey
AY, αυ	av/af	av or af
EI, ει	i	long i, exactly like ι or η
EY, ευ	ev/ef	ev or ef
OI, οι	i	long i, exactly like ι or η
OY, ου	ou	ou as in tourist
ΓΓ, γγ	ng	ng as in angle
ΓΚ, γκ	g/ng	g at start of a word, ng in the middle
ΜΠ, μπ	b/mb	b at start of a word, mb in the middle
ΝΤ, ντ	d/nd	d at start of a word, nd in the middle
ΤΣ, τσ	ts	ts as in hits
ΤΖ, τζ	tz	dg as in judge

Words and phrases

ESSENTIALS

Hello	Hérete
Good morning	Kalí méra
Good evening	Kalí spéra
Goodnight	Kalí níkhta
Goodbye	Adhío
yes	né
certainly	málista
no	óhi
please	parakaló
okay, agreed	endáksi
Thank you (very much)	Efharistó (polí)
I (don't) understand	(Dhen) katalavéno
Excuse me, do you speak English?	Parakaló, mípos miláte angliká?
Sorry/excuse me	Signómi
today	símera
tomorrow	ávrio
more	perisótero
less	ligótero
a little	lígo
a lot	polí
big/small	megálo/mikró
cheap/expensive	ftinó/akrivó
hot/cold	zestó/krío
with/without	mazí/horís
quickly/slowly	grígora/sigá
Mr/Mrs/Miss	Kírios/Kiría/ Dhespinís

to eat/drink	trógo/píno
bakery	foúrnos, psomádhiko
pharmacy	farmakío
post office	tahidhromío
stamps	gramatósima
petrol station	venzinádhiko
bank	trápeza
money	leftá/hrímata
toilet	toualéta
police	astinomía
doctor	iatrós
hospital	nosokomío

QUESTIONS

To ask a question, start with parakaló, then name the thing you want in an interrogative tone.

May I have a kilo of oranges?	Parakaló, éna kiló portokália?
where?	pou?
how?	pos?
how many?	póssi/pósses?
how much?	póso?
when?	póte?
why?	yatí?
at what time...?	ti óra...?
what is/which is...?	ti íne/pió íne..?
how much (does it cost)?	póso káni?
What time does it open/close?	Tí óra aníyi/klíni?

TALKING TO PEOPLE

Greek makes the distinction between the **informal** (esí) and **formal** (esís) second person, as French does with tu and vous. Young people, older people and country people nearly always use esí even with strangers. By far the most common greeting, on meeting and parting, is yá sou/yá sas – literally "health to you".

How are you?	Ti kánis/ti kánete?
I'm fine	Kalá íme
And you?	Ke esís?
What's your name?	Pos se léne?
My name is...	Me léne...
Speak slower, please	Parakaló, miláte pió sigá
How do you say it in Greek?	Pos léyete sta Eliniká?
I don't know	Dhen kséro
See you tomorrow	Tha se dho ávrio
See you soon	Kalí andhámosi
Let's go	Páme
Bon voyage	Kaló taxídhi
Please help me	Parakaló, na me voithíste

ACCOMMODATION

hotel	ksenodhohío
a room	éna dhomátio
We'd like a room for one/two/three people	Parakaló, éna dhomátio ya éna/dhío/tría átoma?
for one/two/three nights	ya mía/dhío/trís vradhiés
with a double bed	me megálo kreváti
with a shower	me doús
hot water	zestó neró
cold water	krío neró
Can I see it?	Boró na to dho?

ON THE MOVE

aeroplane	aeropláno
bus	leoforío
car	aftokínito
motorbike, moped	mihanáki, papáki
taxi	taksí
ship	plío/vapóri/karávi
on foot	me ta pódhia
bus station	praktorío leoforíon
bus stop	stási
harbour	limáni
What time does it leave/arrive?	Ti óra févyi/fthási?
How many kilometres?	Pósa hiliómetra?
How many hours?	Pósses óres?
Where are you going?	Pou pas?
I'm going to...	Páo sto...
I want to get off at...	Thélo na katévo sto...
Can you show me the road to...?	Parakaló, o dhrómos ya...?
Where is the bakery?	Parakaló, o foúrnos?
near	kondá
far	makriá
left	aristerá
right	dheksiá
straight ahead	katefthía
a ticket to...	éna isistírio ya...
a return ticket	éna isistírio me epistrofí

NUMBERS

1	énas/éna/mía
2	dhío
3	trís/tría
4	tésseres/téssera
5	pénde
6	éksi
7	eftá
8	okhtó
9	enyá
10	dhéka
11	éndheka
12	dhódheka
13	dhekatrís
14	dhekatésseres
20	íkosi
21	íkosi éna
30	triánda
40	saránda
50	penínda
60	eksínda
70	evdhomínda
80	ogdhónda
90	enenínda
100	ekató

150	ekatón penínda
200	dhiakóssies/ia
500	pendakóssies/ia
1000	hílies/ia
2000	dhío hiliádhes
1,000,000	éna ekatomírio
first	próto
second	dhéftero
third	tríto

TIME AND DAYS OF THE WEEK

Monday	Dheftéra
Tuesday	Tríti
Wednesday	Tetárti
Thursday	Pémpti
Friday	Paraskeví
Saturday	Sávato
Sunday	Kiriakí
What time is it?	Ti óra íne?
One/two/three o'clock	Mía/dhío/trís óra/ óres
Twenty to four	Tésseres pará íkosi
Five past seven	Eftá ke pénde
Half past eleven	Éndheka ke misí
half-hour	misí óra
quarter-hour	éna tétarto

MONTHS AND SEASONS

January	Yennáris
February	Fleváris
March	Mártis
April	Aprílis
May	Maios
June	Ioúnios
July	Ioúlios
August	Ávgoustos
September	Septémvris
October	Októvrios
November	Noémvris
December	Dhekémvris
summer schedule	Therinó dhromolóyio
winter schedule	Himerinó dhromolóyio

Food and drink glossary

BASICS

aláti	salt
avgá	eggs
boútero	butter
fayitó	food
froúto	fruit
(horís) ládhi	(without) oil
hortofágos	vegetarian
katálogo/menoú	menu
kréas	meat
ládhi, eleóladho	olive oil
lahaniká	vegetables
lemóni	lemon
o logariasmós	the bill
mahyéri	knife
méli	honey
neró	water
pipéri	pepper
piroúni	fork
potíri	glass
psári(a)	fish
psomí	bread
koutáli	spoon
saláta	salad
sídi	vinegar
thalassiná	seafood
tyrí	cheese
yiaoúrti	yoghurt
záhari	sugar

COOKING TERMS

lemonáto	baked with lemon and oil
makaronádha	any pasta-based dish
psitó	roasted
skáras	grilled
sti soúvla	spit-roasted
sto foúrno	baked/roast
tiganitó	pan-fried
tis óras	grilled/fried to order
yemistá	stuffed (squid, vegetables, etc)

STARTERS, SALADS AND MEZÉDHES

angourodomáta saláta	cucumber and tomato salad
avgolémono	egg and lemon soup
bouréki	courgette/zucchini, potato and cheese pie

bekri mezé	pork chunks in red sauce
cochlí	snails
dákos	barley rusks soaked in oil and tomato,
dolmádhes	stuffed vine leaves
domatosaláta	tomato salad
eliés	olives
fasoládha	bean soup
fáva	purée of split peas with onion
horiátiki (salatá)	Greek salad (with olives, feta, etc)
kalitsoúnia	pies filled with mizíthra cheese
keftédhes	meatballs
kolokythákia tiganitá	courgette/zucchini slices fried in batter
kolokythakeftedhes	courgette/zucchini balls (fried)
kolokithoánthi yemistá	stuffed courgette/zucchini flowers
melitzanosaláta	aubergine/eggplant dip
melitzánes tiganités	aubergine/eggplant slices fried in batter
pikiliá	selection of mezédhes
saganáki	fried cheese
soúpa	soup
spanakópita/ spanakopitakia	spinach pies/small spinach pies
taramósalata	fish roe pâté
tsalingaria	snails
tyrokafteri	cheese dip with chilli
tyrópita/tyropitákia	cheese pies/small cheese pies
tzatzíki	yoghurt and cucumber dip
yígandes	white haricot beans

VEGETABLES

angináres	artichokes
angoúri	cucumber
bámies	okra
briám	ratatouille
domátes	tomatoes
fakés	lentils
fasolákia	green beans
hórta	greens (usually wild)
imám bayaldí	stuffed, oven-baked aubergine/eggplant
karóto	carrot
kolokithákia	courgette/zucchini
koukiá	broad beans
kremídhia	onions
láhano	cabbage
ladhéra	vegetables stewed/baked in oil
maroúli	lettuce
melitzána	aubergine/eggplant
papoutsákia	stuffed aubergine/eggplant
patátes	potatoes
piperiés	peppers
radhíkia	wild chicory
rízi/piláfi	rice
saláta	salad
spanáki	spinach
yemistés	stuffed vegetables

MEAT AND POULTRY

arní	lamb
biftéki	hamburger
brizóla	pork or beef chop
hlriló	pork
keftédhes	meatballs
kokorétsi	liver/offal kebab
kotópoulo	chicken
kounéli	rabbit
loukánika	spicy sausages
moskhári	veal
moussaká	aubergine/eggplant, potato and mince pie
païdhákia	lamb chops
papoutsáki	meat-stuffed aubergine/eggplant
pastítsio	macaroni baked with meat
patsás	tripe soup, often served at Easter
psaronéfri	pork tenderloin medallions
sikóti	liver
souvláki	grilled kebab
stifádho	meat stew with tomato and onion

tsoutsoukákia	meatballs in tomato sauce
vodhinó	beef
yíros	doner kebab; sliced, spit-roasted seasoned lamb
youvétsi	meat casserole

FISH AND SEAFOOD

ahini	sea urchins; the roe is eaten as ahinosálata
astakós	lobster
bakaliáros	cod or hake
barbóunia	red mullet
fagrí	sea bream
garídhes	prawns
gávros	anchovy
glóssa	sole
gópa	bogue
kalamária/ kalamarákia	squid/baby squid
kakaviá	bouillabaisse-style fish stew
koliós	mackerel
lavráki	sea bass
marídhes	whitebait
melanoúri	saddled bream
mýdhia	mussels
okhtapódhi	octopus
sardhélles	sardines
sargós	white bream
sinagrídha	dentex
skáros	parrotfish
skorpína	scorpion fish
soupiá	cuttlefish
strídhia	oysters
tónnos	tuna
tsipoúra	gilt-head bream
xifías	swordfish

DESSERTS, FRUIT AND NUTS

baklavá	honey and nut pastry
bougátsa	creamy cheese pie sprinkled with sugar and cinnamon
fistíkia	pistachio nuts
fráoules	strawberries
galaktobóuriko	custard-cream filo pie
halvás	sesame-based sweetmeat
karidhópita	walnut cake
karpoúzi	watermelon
kataífi	"angel hair" pastry filled with nuts
kéik	cake
kerásia	cherries
loukoumádhes	dough fritters served hot with honey or cinnamon
loukoúmia	Turkish delight
míla	apples
milopita/milopitákia	apple pies
pagotó	ice cream
pastéli	sesame and honey bar
pepóni	melon
portokália	oranges
rizógalo	rice pudding
rodhákino	peach
síka	(dried) figs
stafília	grapes
yaoúrti	yoghurt

DRINKS

bíra	beer
boukáli	bottle
frappé	ice-cold, frothed instant coffee;
gazóza	generic fizzy drink
gála	milk
hýma (krasí)	wine from the barrel
kafé	coffee
koniák	brandy
krasí	wine
áspro	white
mávro/kókkino	red
rosé/kokkinéli	rosé
limonádha	lemonade
metalikó neró	mineral water
neró	water
oúzo	distilled grape spirit
portokaládha	orangeade
potíri	glass
Stiniyássas!	Cheers!
tónik	tonic water
tsáï	tea
tsikoudia/ráki	grappa-style firewater

PUBLISHING INFORMATION

This first edition published April 2011 by **Rough Guides Ltd**

80 Strand, London WC2R 0RL

11, Community Centre, Panchsheel Park, New Delhi 110017, India

Distributed by the Penguin Group

Penguin Books Ltd, 80 Strand, London WC2R 0RL

Penguin Group (USA) 375 Hudson Street, NY 10014, USA

Penguin Group (Australia) 250 Camberwell Road, Camberwell, Victoria 3124, Australia

Penguin Group (NZ) 67 Apollo Drive, Mairangi Bay, Auckland 1310, New Zealand

Rough Guides is represented in Canada by

Tourmaline Editions Inc., 662 King Street West, Suite 304, Toronto, Ontario, M5V 1M7

Typeset in Minion and Din to an original design by Henry Iles and Dan May.

Printed and bound in China

© John Fisher, 2011

Maps © Rough Guides

176pp includes index

A catalogue record for this book is available from the British Library

ISBN 978-1-84836-272-7

The publishers and authors have done their best to ensure the accuracy and currency of all the information in **Pocket Rough Guide Athens**, however, they can accept no responsibility for any loss, injury, or inconvenience sustained by any traveller as a result of information or advice contained in the guide.

1 3 5 7 9 8 6 4 2

MIX
Paper from
responsible sources
FSC™ C018179
www.fsc.org

ROUGH GUIDES CREDITS

Text editor: Natasha Foges

Layout: Nikhil Agarwal

Cartography: Katie Lloyd-Jones

Picture editor: Sarah Cummins

Photographers: Chris Christoforou and Michelle Grant

Production: Rebecca Short

Proofreader: Helen Castell

Cover design: Nicole Newman, Dan May and Chloë Roberts

THE AUTHOR

John Fisher co-authored the first edition of the *Rough Guide to Greece* – the first Rough Guide ever – and has been inextricably linked with Rough Guides ever since. He lives in South London with his wife and two sons.

ACKNOWLEDGEMENTS

John Fisher: Thanks, as ever, are due to far more people than can be listed here, but above all to James Monteith, Kate Donnelly, Nick Edwards, Dorina Stathopoulou, Yannis Assimacopoulos, everyone at Rough Guides and all of you who wrote in with updates and suggestions – keep 'em coming. Above all to A and the two Js for putting up with it all.

Chris Christoforou: A very big thank you to Sarah Cummins for the great opportunity; to Nick Edwards for sharing his expert knowledge; to all the amazing Greeks who extended their welcome; and to my dear family in Athens. Dimitri, thankyou for being my guide off the beaten track, and for climbing to the top of Filopáppou with me, carrying my tripod in the middle of the night so I could take photos of the Acropolis.

HELP US UPDATE

We've gone to a lot of effort to ensure that the first edition of the **Pocket Rough Guide Athens** is accurate and up-to-date. However, things change – places get "discovered", opening hours are notoriously fickle, restaurants and rooms raise prices or lower standards. If you feel we've got it wrong or left something out, we'd like to know, and if you can remember the address, the price, the hours, the phone number, so much the better.

Please send your comments with the subject line "**Pocket Rough Guide Athens Update**" to ⓔ mail@roughguides.com. We'll credit all contributions and send a copy of the next edition (or any other Rough Guide if you prefer) for the very best emails.

Find more travel information, connect with fellow travellers and book your trip on ⓦ www .roughguides.com

PHOTO CREDITS

All images © Rough Guides except the following:
Front cover The Erechtheion © 2010 photolibrary.com
Back cover Tourists viewing the Parthenon under restoration © Atlantide Phototravel/ Corbis
p.1 Siphnian Treasury, Delphi © René Mattes/ Hemis/Corbis
p.2 Porch of the Caryatids © Barbar Walton/ epa/Corbis
p.4 Poseidon statue, National Archeological Museum © René Mattes/Hemis/Corbis
p.5 View of the Acropolis from Filopáppou Hill © Atlantide Phototravel/Corbis
p.12 New Acropolis Museum © Atlantide Phototravel/Corbis
p.22 The Klityon Gallery, Acropolis Museum © Georgios Kefalas/Keystone/Corbis
p.23 Benáki Museum, courtesy of Benáki Museum
p.24 Pláka fish market © Kaos03/SIME/ 4corners
p.30 Temple of Athena Nike © Bettmann/Corbis

p.34 New Acropolis Museum © Georgios Kefalas/Keystone/Corbis
p.35 Herodes Atticus Theatre © Wolfgang Kaehler/Corbis
p.38 Stoa of Attalos © Orestis Panagiotou/ epa/Corbis
p.110 Panathenaic Stadium © Robert Harding World Imagery/Corbis
p.131 Aráhova © Paul A Souders/Corbis
p.132 Tholos at Delphi © Miles Ertman/Corbis
p.133 Temple of Apollo, Delphi © Perry Mastrovito/Corbis
p.134 Temple of Apollo, Corinth © Bettmann/ Corbis
p.137 Lion Gate, Mycenae © Pete Saloutos/ Corbis
p.139 Ýdhra © Jose Fuste Raga/Corbis
p.140 Ýdhra waterfront © Jon Hicks/Corbis
p.142 *Herodion* roof garden, courtesy of the *Herodion* hotel
p.150 Changing of the Guard, the Voulí © Allan Baxter/Getty

Index

Maps are marked in **bold**.

SO NOW WE'VE TOLD YOU
ABOUT THE THINGS NOT TO
MISS, THE BEST PLACES TO
STAY, THE TOP RESTAURANTS,
THE LIVELIEST BARS AND THE
MOST SPECTACULAR SIGHTS,
IT ONLY SEEMS FAIR TO
TELL YOU ABOUT THE BEST
TRAVEL INSURANCE AROUND

WorldNomads.com
keep travelling safely

RECOMMENDED BY ROUGH GUIDES

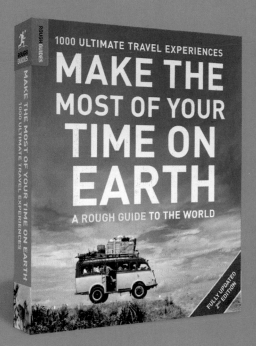